MW00612642

Thirsting for Joy
Desert Journey
Healing the Earth

Book 2 in the Thirsting Series
Sequel to Thirsting for a Raindrop

Lyneah Marks

Body
Soul &
Angels
Publishing

Thirsting for Joy
First Edition
Copyright © 2021 by Body, Soul & Angels Publishing

ISBN: 978-0-9889827-3-4

Dedication page.

I dedicate this book to all

who follow your heart's spiritual calling

and find joy in doing so.

Foreword

It has taken a long time to write the sequel to Thirsting for a Raindrop and much life has happened during that time. When I finally felt ready to write this one, it flowed quickly. I do hope you enjoy it. I hope it's been worth the wait. May you find inspiration and encouragement in these stories to help you live your life even more fully. If I can do it, so can you.

Acknowledgments

Many people have encouraged me to write this and I thank them all. Especially my husband and editor, Marc Harper, who continues to love and support me in amazing ways. Allysha Bounds, a dear friend and colleague who encourages me regularly. Jennifer Martin, my niece who is a wonderful listener. She caught redundancies, offered word alternatives and asked important questions for clarification. Fonda Joyce who never pushed and let me know she loved me daily. To all my guides visible and energetic. To all who read this and feel inspired I am grateful, for you fulfill the purpose of this book.

COVER ART STORY

It was a gorgeous day in the Potomac Highlands of West Virginia: 72 degrees, sunny, slightly breezy, a few wispy clouds floating overhead. I held my draw knife over the cedar log resting in the draw table I built and watched the bark strips fall away revealing the deep color of red. The aroma of cedar filled my nostrils. I love working with beautiful wood and this cedar was gorgeous. ! I looked up at the sky and felt, *"it doesn't get better than this!"* A rush of joy escaped from my heart.and floated like a beautiful cloud in front of me. Suddenly, a hummingbird appeared and hovered close enough to touch, directly in front of me. We looked each other in the eye. It stayed and stayed hovering close. I opened to its joy. It felt as if the hummingbird was asking,

"What are you doing with my energy: the energy of joy?"

Lyneah Marks
www.bodysoulandangels.com
Lyneah@bodysoulandangels.com

Table of Contents

Chapter One Westward Bound 1

Chapter Two New Orleans 9

Chapter Three Nobody Knows 15

Chapter Four The Sun Is Ris 19

Chapter Five Doggone It 25

Chapter Six Doing Desert 31

Chapter Seven Gems and Minerals and Fossils, Oh My!..............35

Chapter Eight Cool, Clear, Water 39

Chapter Nine Two AM 43

Chapter Ten Cocaine 45

Chapter Eleven Being...49

Chapter Twelve Teec Nos Pos 53

Chapter Thirteen Mysterious Stone 59

Chapter Fourteen Work Search...63

Chapter Fifteen Embracing Worthiness and Joy..........................67

Chapter Sixteen The Elephant in the Room.................................71

Chapter Seventeen Crystal Clear 75

Chapter Eighteen Bi-Coastal 77

Chapter Nineteen Lessons in Wisdom.......................................79

Chapter Twenty No Happy Ending 83

Chapter Twenty-One Flamingo Paste..87

Chapter Twenty-Two Hyundai 89

Chapter Twenty-Three Making the Wheel 91

Chapter Twenty-Four In Search of Enlightenment 93

Chapter Twenty-Five Ceremonies 99

Chapter Twenty-Six The King's Castle 101

Chapter Twenty-Seven Have Sagittarius will Travel 103

Chapter Twenty-Eight Monkey Business 111

Chapter Twenty-Nine Flipping 115

Chapter Thirty Bliss & Ecstasy 121

Chapter Thirty-One Mysterious Disappearances 125

Chapter Thirty-Two Manifesting Smooth Air 131

Chapter Thirty-Three A New School of Healing 135

Chapter Thirty-Four The North Rim 139

Chapter Thirty-Five Squash Blossom 147

Chapter Thirty-Six After Albuquerque 155

Chapter Thirty-Seven Flopped 157

Chapter Thirty-Eight Stuck in the Mud 161

Chapter Thirty-Nine Heading Home 165

Chapter Forty Hugged by a House? 169

Chapter Forty-One Interview 175

About the Author 183

A SPECIAL BONUS GIFT FROM LYNEAH 185

TESTIMONIALS 187

Chapter One
Westward Bound

Ms. Carley, my beautiful Sheltie-Australian Shepherd mix, laid her head on the console between us. She was happy to be traveling. She had not always loved travel but thanks to a lovely young girl she now did.

*****

Packing for a Body, Mind and Spirit Expo in Charlotte, NC, I was guided to take a plastic angel necklace with me. Briefly, I wondered,

"W*hy take this plastic thing to a metaphysical show?*" It had been a gift, a little cartoon-like and I've never been fond of plastic. It was not the sort of thing I would buy nor what I would wear and certainly not something I would expect to sell at such a fair but I took it as guided and placed it on the table among the various crystals and beaded jewelry I was selling. To my eye it looked out of place.

I didn't feel entirely well and I had recently lost my connection to my main guide, Uriel. I felt a bit empty, alone, even lost without him. I realized I had become co-dependent on an archangel and I didn't know what to do about it! When I first learned that my guide was Uriel, I said,

"The Archangel Uriel?"

"Yes," came the calm, simple answer.

"Go away. I am not ready to work with Archangels. I've just started working with angels and am still getting used to that." I did not feel worthy of working with an Archangel.

"Get over yourself. I've been working with you for weeks." Was the clear response. I walked around that entire day rather mind-blown repeating in my head,

"I've been told to get over myself by an Archangel!!!"

I had gone fairly quickly from unworthy to co-dependent and I missed his presence terribly. This was heavy on my heart and I feared my healing career was possibly over. I didn't want to be here at this expo but I had booked it months ago and it was a strong guidance that told me to participate.

Unloading was a disaster. The cart they gave me got hung up on a joint in the concrete and threw half my inventory off, breaking some major pieces. Reloading in a busy hallway was a major task.

Debra, my partner for this show, was already there and working. I was late. After I got set up, I went to the bathroom. On the way back, Matt, a big bear of an intuitive reader grabbed me and started to work on me with a crystal wand.

"Uriel has gone to the underworld to do some work. He asked me to tell you. You cannot follow him there. You are to open to other guides. Use discernment and ask for those who are right action to work with you each time and you will develop relationships with many masters. Go, work your booth, there is someone coming for you." He released his hold on me physically and energetically. I returned to our booth surprised and grateful. I continued to place crystals on my half of the table.

I looked up into the clear, translucent blue eyes of a ten-year-old girl. She pointed shyly at the angel necklace with a questioning look. I nodded and said,

"Please try it on."

Her response was a lovely smile that lit up her face and the space around it. When she put the necklace on, it transformed into something special and I knew it was hers. Her love and appreciation transformed it into something beautiful.

"That's yours," I said in admiration, glad for the necklace to have an appreciative home.

"How much is it?" she asked in a soft gentle voice.

"Oh, nothing. It's yours."

2

"You know she's an animal communicator, don't you?" said her mother, leaning around from behind.

"Really?" Mom nodded. Her brown-haired daughter stood erect but shy holding the necklace with joy.

"Could you try communicating with my dog, Carley?" she nodded and closed her eyes in concentration in this noisy fair atmosphere. It took a shorter time than I expected and she looked at me and nodded her head confirming contact.

"Please ask her why she goes crazy whenever we take rides in the country." Carley was a rescue and I only knew part of her history. When I first got her, she jumped into my car and looked at me with a face that said, "*What are you waiting for?*" We had bonded almost immediately. Lately though, she jumped nervously side to side in the back seat whenever we drove out into the country.

After another pause for internal concentration the girl said,

"She is afraid you are going to abandon her in the country like the other people did."

"Please assure her that I plan to keep her but if I ever need to give her away, I would make sure it would be to a good home."

After yet another pause, she nodded her head, opened her eyes and said,

"She understands."

"Thank you." I said hopefully.

After that Carley stopped jumping around nervously on our drives. She had been abandoned on a road pregnant and there's no way this girl in a city three hours away could have known that. I became less skeptical of animal communicators that day.

*****

"Hello?" I answered my cell phone.

"Hi, how far have you gotten?" asked Marc.

"I have just left my daughter and her boyfriend in Atlanta. Can you believe she's now smoking? My daughter, who, as a child used to

3

break my cigarettes and throw them in the trash is now smoking!!! The one who badgered me into quitting!"

"OK but how was your visit other than that?"

"It was OK. Now I'm heading Southwest and the sky has a large feather cloud which is pointing West."

"That's nice to hear. Work is kind of busy today, I've got to go but if you need me, call."

"I will. I have Jennifer Berezan and Friends' *Praises for the World* on the CD player and I'm meditating on Earth healing as I drive. It's quite wonderful."

"Good to hear. How's Carley doing?"

"She's fine…more than fine, she's content and happy. She loves our walks and loves having me with her 24/7. She'd rather be in my lap but I've been clear she needs to stay on the front seat on her side. She always has new smells which makes her happy and she's eating well."

"I look forward to seeing both of you in a few days."

"Yes, I plan to drive pretty much straight through but I will not rush or push it. When I get tired, I'll stop and I'm stopping about every two hours to walk Carley and stretch my legs."

"I want you here in one piece. Please take your time and be safe," said Marc sincerely.

"My plan exactly…" a brief yummy intimate silence followed. I realized he was at work and couldn't talk freely. "Talk with you when you are off work. I'm still two hours ahead of you in time today."

"I'll call on my way home from work but if you need me, call," said Marc.

*****

Marc and I met several years ago at a Jean Houston Mystery School in New York and struck up a friendship. He had since left his wife of 28 years and moved to Arizona. After the separation was definite, he had expressed romantic interest and I had told him I was not interested in anything of the sort. I was not attracted and thought he would be a project. Valorie, a lovely West Texas RN and student of my Body, Soul and Angels Healing Classes, had invited me to visit Phoenix. She said, in her sweet West Texas accent,

"I need my teacher out here."

"You live in an oven," was my response. But one day she called and said she was buying me a ticket to Phoenix as my birthday present. She wanted to show me how wonderful Arizona was. I agreed I would come but warned her she would be disappointed at my feelings toward the desert.

"I will only come in October, not before."

"Done - I'll get your ticket for October first. It'll be a weeklong stay because of price but I will have only four days off for us to travel. You'll have to make other plans for the other days. You can use my Jeep if you drive me to work."

"That's fine. I want to tour Taliesin West, Frank Lloyd Wright's western school."

"Oh, that's not far from me. It's near Scottsdale."

I had not consulted the internet weather forecast. I thought it would be cool in October. When I arrived a dry hot blast of air hit me when I walked out the Sky Harbor Airport door. It was 105°F!!! My sinuses were not amused. I immediately turned around, reentered the air conditioning and looked for the nearest drugstore to stock up on Evian water spray and a nasal spray to help my sinuses adjust. I had already packed tons of sunscreen and moisturizer.

"*I should have said December,*" I thought with a flood of regret.

Valorie tried her best to show me around Arizona: Sedona, Jerome, Flagstaff riding up to 10,000 ft. Mt. Humphreys where it was 34°F, topping the trip off with the aptly named Grand Canyon at dawn, 'the greatest earth on show'.

"Isn't it beautiful?" Val asked on our drive back down I-17. She was most disappointed when I said,

"Yes, it is. May I please go back to where the trees have green leaves and the rivers have water?" I have never felt safe in the desert. I simply don't know how to survive there. Not just dry, it was hostile. You must avoid cholla cacti -- give them a wide birth because their quills jump at you if you get too close - or at least that's the story. Dogs that did not respect the berth required spent painful hours having barbed quills removed. One person told me of his adventure having them removed from his leg and he still praised the desert! Rattlesnakes and scorpions added to a frightening landscape.

Knowing Valorie only had four days before returning to her 12+ hour shifts, I called Marc and told him I'd like to see him but emphasized I was not interested in anything romantic.

"It would do me no pleasure to violate any of your boundaries," was his considered response.

"Really good answer!" I thought. Impressed, I felt safe. I was able to establish clear boundaries and he respected them. We had a good base of friendship developed at the once a month year-long Mystery School and in phone calls since. I had encouraged him to get out and have some social contact outside of work. He picked me up at Valorie's and we greeted with a friendly hug. Val declined joining us, too busy preparing for her marathon hospital shift.

We had a great time at a modern, tasty, large-windowed Thai restaurant. He took me back to Val's and I slept well that night. The next morning Marc picked me up early and we drove around the perimeter of the Valley and West stopping in at a Starbucks in a town called Surprise. Marc ordered Chai tea lattes for us while I went to the lady's room. As I came out of the bathroom, it was like someone had quite suddenly flipped a switch. I saw Marc quite differently. I realized I was in love with him! I was shocked at this shift and took a few seconds to feel its reality. Not able to shake it off, I slowly traversed the room in something of a trance, eyes locked, Marc put down the cups in anticipation, enfolded me in his arms and I kissed him directly on his lips.

"It would appear you've changed your mind," he said with a look full of questions. I smiled and we kissed again unaware of people around us. My heart soared, my brain said,

"WHAT???"

*****

6

Now, only 3 ½ months later, here I was moving to Arizona based on spiritual guidance leaving my home of 17 years.

In my meditation on the plane returning to North Carolina I heard, *"Your support has moved to Arizona. If you want to feel supported, you must move."*

"I don't do desert," was my response but I knew I had to start packing. Many truck loads taken to the thrift shop, yard sales and tossing later, here I was moving with my dog and what I could fit into Goldie, my beloved Mazda 626, driving cross country. I had no job prospects. I only knew two people in the entire state and one was a very new relationship. Marc was an unknown quantity in a way. We had never lived close to each other. When we met in upstate New York in 2002, he lived near Boston and I lived in the Triangle area of North Carolina (a two-day drive). He had visited once in NC on his way to Florida. Since his move to Arizona, we had a brief day's encounter in Mt. Shasta, California with the meditation group I was attending. On Panther Meadows, Marc sang the song he had written for me. We had talked by phone occasionally and developed a friendship until the visit to Valorie.

We had had a wonderful dinner the night before Surprise. They were all special encounters but a few meetings do not a relationship make, right? I had also never lived with Valorie and while I suspected it could work out, I was also unsure of that situation. Friendships can be ruined by living together. This move made no logical sense; it was a move of my heart listening to my intuition. My twenty-one-year-old daughter and her boyfriend, both grounded in logic, had pointed out all their reservations over dinner and I thought,

"We live our lives under our parent's scrutiny the first years. After that, do we have to live under the scrutiny of our children?"

Alexandrea concluded with the question,

"Are you CRAZY?"

Good question.

I should have been filled with joy and to some degree I did have joy but it was tainted with apprehension. So many question marks.

7

So many unknowables and at this point I allowed them to tarnish my joy.

Chapter Two
New Orleans

"Hi, how are you? How's the trip going?" called Marc on his way to work.

"Beautiful. It's sunny and mild. Ms. Carley is doing so well. She's such good company. There's another large feather cloud pointing Southwest in the sky today. It's as if I'm being reassured this is the right move."

"Well, I'm glad it's bringing you this way. I so look forward to seeing you again. What mile marker are you at now?" After some figuring, Marc estimated the time we would arrive in New Orleans, which had been calling to me. I was aware of a past life there and suspected this had something to do with it. I remembered being in a deep trance state, perusing the Akashic Records:

My skin is black and I am in a ship. It is very crowded and it smells terrible. Now I'm on the selling block at Jackson Square and men are touching me in most inappropriate ways. My hands are tied behind my back and I am unable to object. I have seen others beaten because they objected. I could tell I was young, tall, beautiful and buxom. I was purchased by a man I disliked from the beginning. His smile was crooked and so was his heart. There was no escape. I had to go with him to find out what my fate would bring. The next thing I remember is crying into the lap of Big Mammy who was petting my hair and singing,

"Nobody Knows the Troubles I've Seen…"

"Try it, baby, it helps ease the pain. Sing with me," Instructed Bertha. She would say,

9

"Honey, if you was fat like me they wouldn't bother you none," as she rocked me to soothe my soul. I was the most attractive slave so I drew the most attention from the men-- attention I wasn't interested in. Some of them liked that I didn't like it, it seemed to turn them on, so I learned to be neutral. I often left my body during the act and hid in the corner of the room watching myself being taken. My freedom was in not giving them my orgasm. It was the one thing I could control. This made some of them angry. I didn't care.

While reviewing this lifetime I started to feel a victim and I know that doesn't help. Getting a hold of myself I yelled out loud,

"Why did I choose this lifetime?"

"To develop strength of will," came the clear, concise answer.

"Why do I need so 'friggen' much strength of will?????" I was shown a tableau of many situations in my life which had required strength of will, including the logging incident[1]. After the tableau, the additional message was,

"This is one of three lifetimes it took you to develop the strength of will you have now. And your life isn't over yet."

"Wonderful." I thought with some melancholy and apprehension.

Recently, I had returned to the Akashic records to see this lifetime and learned that the plantation owner was a man who came into a company I worked for (current lifetime) as the new President. I had always been uncomfortable around him and, my two 'friends' suggested I might have an affair with him to help them get rid of him! The idea made me ill. Now I knew why.

I asked what else I needed to know about this lifetime and this is what I was shown...

Near the end of the Civil War the plantation owner had raped me again, tied me naked to the cross beams of an outbuilding and whipped me until my back bled. He tied my hands over my head so I faced the empty main house. I slumped, exhausted from the

---

[1] See Thirsting for a Raindrop or search on www.bodysoulandangels.com/blog

beatings. I could feel the blood trickling down my back. He had moved his family and possessions to a safer location and was about to burn this one to keep it from falling into Union hands. He carefully poured gasoline around the lonely house. He looked back at me often as if to say he had won in the end. He always wanted me to give him my orgasm and I did not, never, especially not now. When he finished surrounding the house with gasoline, he trailed some to the outbuilding where I was tied, giving me one final look. He turned his back on me, walked to the house, lit a match and the 'whoof' of the fire caused the horses to rear, whinny and nervously pull at their ties. As he hopped onto the wagon the horses were more than willing to oblige him with a quick exit. He never looked back.

I watched the building burn. It would be some time before it came to me but I welcomed it. I was happy to be done with the rapes from the entire neighborhood of men. I watched myself pass out from exhaustion, pain and hopelessness. Watching from outside the scene, I noticed a different buckboard wagon. A Union soldier found me, cut me down, found my pulse, got an army issue wool blanket and wrapped me in it as gently as he could but I winced through the coma at the pain. He placed me unconscious on his wagon's buckboard and drove to a cave.

Some days later I woke briefly while he was applying a soothing liquid on my back. He was a Union Doctor and I watched him, from outside the vision, walk the meadows in search of healing herbs. He carefully picked the ones he needed and created preparations for my back and soups to bring me strength. He patiently helped me back to health. I didn't talk for a long time, confused by this man's kind actions. What did he want? The only white men I had known had not been kind to say the least.

"Ain't you gonna fuck me?" were the first words I spoke huddled in the blanket in a corner of the cave.

"No, I'm not like that," he responded from the fire in the center of the room.

"All White mens fuck me," I said definitively.

"Not me," was his simple reply.

11

As I became stronger, he left some days for quite a while but always came back to feed me. One day I was wailing "Nobody Knows the Troubles I've Seen" and when he appeared at the cave entrance, backlit by the bright sunlight. I stopped singing abruptly. It was the first time he heard me sing. He looked at me long and hard and then walked over and gave me the soft light blue cotton dress draped over his arm. My back had healed enough to tolerate clothing. The soft cotton felt good on my back and the dress was lovely, nicer than anything I'd had.

"Thank you." I said simply overwhelmed at his kindness. "How can I pay you?" my eyes filling with tears.

"No need," he paused. "I was so weary from all the bloodshed of this war I needed a break from all that kind of doctoring. This has been a pleasure to help you heal. I'm so sorry for how that man treated you. I can only imagine all you've been through."

I nodded eyes wide. Kindness was not what I had come to experience from white men.

"Not all white men are like that," he looked to make sure I understood this possibility. "I heard you singing. You are quite good."

"Oh, that's nothin', it's just how ol' mammy taught me to bury my sorrow. Don't know where they took her."

"She taught you well. Please sing for me a bit."

I felt somewhat removed from the scene now and watched as she sang for him and he realized she could make a living in New Orleans as a singer. She was good, so much soul in that music, so much pain. It was moving. He was moved. When she was well enough, he took her to New Orleans, set her up with a job and a room.

"You have to go?" she asked.

He nodded.

"You'll be OK here. I must face the end of the war and find out what I have to do. They'll want to know where I went. I have much explaining to do."

"Are you in trouble 'cause of me?"

"No," he looked down in a sad way and continued, "'cause of me."

"How…" she searched for words and composure, *"how can I thank you?"* her eyes filled with tears.
 "Live a good rest of your life."
 "Will I see you again?"
 He shrugged in response and she jumped at him and hugged him hard before he could object. He didn't pull back.
 The vision began to fade and I felt her gratitude flood my heart space and my eyes well with tears in the present time. Before the vision completely faded, I asked,
 "Do I know this Union Doctor in the present lifetime?"

The answer came quickly and clearly,

"Marc."

Chapter Three
Nobody Knows

"Hello, my love, how are you doing?"

"Hi Marc, I've just settled into a room and told Carley this is our temporary home."

"Did you bring her food in?"

"Yes, first thing - and her bed and toys too. She knows we will be staying here tonight. We had a nice long walk and she's ready to sleep. I think she'll be ok in this room."

"Are you ready to head into town?"

"Yes and I brought a spare battery to make sure we stay connected."

"Good idea. Where do you want to have dinner?"

"In the French Quarter somewhere, where do you recommend?"

"Brennan's on Royal Street, the great tourist restaurant that also happens to be really good, might work."

I had to drive around the Quarter several times running light energy before I felt I could feel comfortable getting out of the car. Marc directed me in getting to a good parking space near the restaurant. Marc had not only had lived here but he has a photographic memory of streets and addresses and highway numbers, etc. (But, full disclosure, he can't remember where to put the grater in the kitchen!) Being the weekend, the waiting line stretched down the street.

"I'm too hungry to wait that long. Let me look around."

I found a nearby restaurant and had a lovely Cajun dinner. Afterward, with my headset on, Marc began guiding me around the famous Bourbon Street. Since it was January and it was still early evening, it was not crowded but had a slow, steady flow of people. On a side street I went into a trance meditation state and because Marc was my anchor, I could open to what Spirit wanted to show me…

I stopped suddenly in front of a house, seeing a woman being thrown out of her apartment with her suitcase coming after her, giving her additional bruises. People behind me almost ran into me and grumbled as they went around. They could not see what was so real in front of me. I saw the slave girl, now a singer, being thrown out of an apartment house with the landlord yelling,

"No rent, no space. I ain't no charity."

I got a 'download' of information that told me she made plenty of money but did not understand the value of money nor how to manage it. As a slave, money was unfamiliar. She was a soft touch, giving it to anyone who asked and word got around. When it came time to pay rent, she didn't have the money. After being thrown out of several rooms, someone kind took her in. After determining she had no mathematical skills, not even basic addition, he told her,

"You have to be paid in ones. Tell your boss to pay you only in ones. Cash out your tips and get all ones at the end of the night. I'll make the marks for how many ones you need for rent in this envelope, for food in this one…" the lesson went on. *"Once you have all those dollars put away, then you can save the rest for something special, you can spend it or give it to others if you want. You must take care of yourself first before giving money away and most of those guys who ask for money will only spend it on drink. They are not worth it and it doesn't really help them."*

I stood in this one spot while I watched the holographs and received the information, astonished at the clarity and detail. A young man on his cell phone bumped into me and brought me back to the present.

Marc continued to guide me on the phone. At an open window café, I saw a drummer playing on a small, raised stage. The scene changed while I stood still. In a flash, a beautiful black woman was wailing the blues - and she was good. The scene flashed back and forth between the drummer present in this time and my former self singing post-civil war. A waitress asked if I wanted a seat. I shook my head no not wanting to talk and break the spell. I continued watching with wonder at the scene slipping back and forth between present time and the blues singer of more than 100 years ago. The large tip jar in front of her was stuffed to the brim with bills. The depth of her soulfulness was impressive and she drew a large appreciative crowd. After some time passed, I turned from this scene and started to walk past a series of psychic readers. A gypsy reader sitting at a candle-lit card table offered me a reading. Our eyes connected and I thought it would be interesting but not wanting to break this trance state I said, "Not now, thank you."

Next, I found myself on Jackson's Square where I backed up to the black wrought iron gates of the majestic 18th Century St. Louis Cathedral. Marc reassured me he was on the phone and holding space for me, so I relaxed again into vision. I saw the square before me in present time. The bright sun was setting. I was learning how to bring the visions on by shifting something in my thinking. The square started to morph into Pre-Civil War times. A slave auction came into focus. I watched as people were treated like cattle. It was uncomfortable to watch. Then I saw spirits who had been sold still lingering here. Working with my angel guides, I listened to their stories and helped them to let go and cross over. This process was familiar to me; I had been doing it for years. But the presence of the visions was stronger than I'd experienced as an adult. Tears of joy were streaming down my face as I saw souls being released from this place.

"Nobody knows the troubles I've seen," rang out a loud, strong baritone voice. I turned in the direction of the voice.

"Nobody knows but Jesus…" continued a short black man standing erect wearing a loose, worn, over-sized coat. The overhead garage door spotlight and architectural arch set a dramatic frame giving the effect that he was standing in a stage spotlight. I realized it was now dark. He continued into *Swing Low Sweet Chariot* as if he were singing to a grand audience. I would not have been surprised to hear someone say, "Print it, that's a take."

Finally, back at the motel with Marc's directional, energetic and emotional support, for which I was enormously grateful, I greeted and walked Ms. Carley. Then the healing work started and I physically shook at the emotions releasing as I finally relaxed. Marc's openness, gentle guidance, lack of judgment and strong holding of space were surprising and welcome. I felt lucky to have him in my life. I also felt the depth of my appreciation for all he did for me as the Union Doctor. My affection for this man was deepening and widening. I had asked for a partner only if it could be a healthy relationship with mutual respect (plus a long list of attributes most of which he seemed to have). This relationship seemed to be heading in the right direction. He accepted me, metaphysics and all.

We carry unresolved energies from past lives and Soul Integration past life healing work opens the door to release these energies. I once worked on a massage client referred by another therapist. He had a spot in his back that would not release with normal massage. A grizzly bear appeared in my vision as I held energy over the spot. Reviewing the lifetime, we managed to effect an energetic release and the pain in the spot left when he forgave the bear and realized why he had chosen that experience.

My current situation was going to take more work than that and the deep ribbons of gratitude flowing toward Marc and the Universe would facilitate it. I turned on a hot shower, stepped inside, welcomed the healing waters and started to wail,

"Nobody knows the troubles I've seen…"

Chapter Four
The Sun Is Ris

"The sun is ris', the sun is set and we ain't out of Texas yet."

I was about to learn just how true this phrase is. Two-plus days to traverse Texas along Interstate 10 is largely boring; however, I was happy to entertain some sameness after the New Orleans experience. I was still a bit shaken and quite tired. After a filling breakfast and a good walk with Ms. Carley, I continued to listen to *Praises for the World*, run light and pet Ms. Carley as I drove following the ever-present westward pointing 'feathers' in the sky.

"Hi love, how are you after yesterday's adventure?" Marc inquired.

"Wow, that was something. I slept deeply, got up early and I'm on the road. It felt like I was being worked on all night. Years ago, a woman told me I was a time traveler. I didn't understand and just filed it away under 'L' for later. Yesterday was the most outrageous experience I've had of that kind. I've had others; they were just little experiences compared to this one and it's because you were there on the phone keeping me somewhat grounded." A rush of gratitude flowed through me again and I remembered this man had saved me in another time as well.

"I don't think I could have found the car without your help. Thank you so much for making me tell you its exact location when I first parked," the gratitude opened to joy. My heart glowed.

"That was pretty amazing and you are welcome. I don't pretend to understand it logically either."

"Yes, it's one thing to read the Akashic Records and see in my mind's eye what happened in another time, it's entirely another to

19

feel like I'm on a holodeck switching back and forth between two times."

"I can only imagine. It was an honor to hold space for you and guide you through the streets I know so well. Where are you now?"

"Trying to stay in this time zone and driving, I just passed Lafayette on my way to Lake Charles where we'll stop to walk."

We chatted for a time talking about everyday things. Then Marc said he had to go and do some shopping.

"I'll call you later. Have a good drive."

I drove in silence now, just allowing the events of yesterday to digest to bring wonder into my soul. I knew of the theories that all things happen at the same time, the thought that we in third dimension are tied by time -- or at least some of us are! – crossed my mind.

Earlier in my life I had earned a Master's Degree and I'd never seen a course offering for time travel. All I had was for references was Sci-Fi and the most outstanding example for me was Dr. Who and his Tardis.

Most Sci-fi involving time travel used a machine. I had none. When the visions and sensations started, all I needed to do was relax and allow and I wondered how I was able to do that? Why didn't this entire experience freak me out? Instead, I found it comforting and when I focused on the souls crossing into the light, being freed, this brought me great joy. My heart soared. I had miles and miles of reasonably bland landscape to ponder, as Douglas Adams put it, 'Life the Universe and EVERYTHING'.

*****

"Hi Marc, I have a question."

"Hi sweet lady, what's your question?"

"Can you direct me to a Whole Foods Store?"

"Where are you now?"

"Past Houston and heading to San Antonio where I plan to stop for the night. I wanted to see the Alamo."

"You are making good time and you just happen to be near one of the largest Whole Foods in the country. You asked at just the right time."

Marc proceeded to give me directions including exit numbers. He was better than my GPS and much friendlier. Afterwards, he got on the internet to double-check himself and found he was correct. What a memory! I can't even tell you the exit number for the house I lived in for ten years (but I can tell you where the grater is supposed to live in the kitchen lol).

I was surprised to hear him say I was making good time. I knew if he made this trip it would have taken half the time. I, however, needed to stop and walk and let my body recover. I was not accustomed to sitting all day. Being a massage therapist for many years, I was used to moving and standing most of the day. Walking with Ms. Carley was a source of joy because she was always ready for an adventure. She was so intelligent she knew to watch for my instructions despite her desire to take off. She only had to be told something once, as long as it did not involve chocolate.

The year I first got Carley, I came home to a scene of Christmas presents strewn throughout the house. They all involved chocolate. A series of gift bags were spread over the house and the chocolate inside every one of them was partially eaten. I think the aluminum foil stopped her from eating them all. I called a friend who was an MD and a dog lover and asked if it would hurt her. She told me what to look for and indicated she would probably have some diarrhea. Carley had no negative effects from eating half of three different chocolate bars. Later I asked an animal communicator to tell her that chocolate is not good for dogs. The communicator asked,

"Do you want to hear what she said?"

"Yes," I responded wondering about her hesitation.

"Are you crazy??????" was her loud response.

The Alamo was interesting and is now off my bucket list. It wasn't open at the time, so I just walked around the periphery and tuned in to what energies were there. A few ghost clearings happened and some shifts of energy but nothing major.

On Marc's recommendation, the San Antonio Riverwalk was delightful and I found an excellent restaurant with outdoor seating which allowed Ms. Carley to be with me. Carley enjoyed the table scraps which were given to reinforce her good behavior. She was such a pretty dog and generally friendly; she often started conversations with other dog lovers. I had several brief friendly exchanges with other travelers and some without their dogs wanting some doggie love. Some pleasant social contact was a welcome change from driving alone.

A long drive later I felt a shift of energy and heard an intuitive, *"GET OFF!"*

I obeyed and exited right away, realizing I had just entered New Mexico. This exit led to the information plaza. Inside, a Native American man stood behind the counter and after hellos I said,

"Are there any hot mineral springs near here?" I had no conscious thought of hot mineral springs and was surprised by my question.

"Well, yes but they are a drive from here."

"How far a drive?"

"Twenty-five miles."

"Well, I've driven nearly 2,000, so I figure 25 more won't hurt me."

He shifted his attitude, turned to the wall behind him, found a brochure and handed it to me. I perused it, called and booked the last cabin with a fenced yard for Ms. Carley.

In the car a flood of joy went through me. I am so grateful to the guides that push me to do things that I love. Hot springs are one of my favorite places to relax and I could use some relaxation and time to further digest the events of New Orleans.

"You are going to have a yard to run in tonight, Ms. Carley."

She snuggled in a little closer feeling my excitement that something good was going to happen. I pet her but restrained her from coming across the console. She was too large for a lap dog in my estimation - but not in hers.

I drove up to Faywood Mineral Springs singing and laughing. I mean up. It turned out to be at the beginning of some seriously steep country. Faywood was on a high plateau near the mountains of Silver City where we picked up food for dinner. A wrong turn or two put us navigating some roads that would rival San Francisco.

The small modern log cabin was adorable, with a kitchen and room for four people or at least two adults and two children. It was no more expensive than some very mediocre motels I'd stayed in along the highway and this one included a full kitchen, access to the hot springs and the fenced yard. I checked to make sure there were no scorpions or unfriendly snakes before letting Ms. Carley run.

"This place is perfect! Thank you, thank you, thank you." I exclaimed to the air. I threw a ball for Carley to chase. Her tail wagging showed her joy. She was happy to be off leash for a change and she romped through the yard with a smile on her face. Her marking did make it look like she had a smile and when her tail was wagging, her eyes expectant, she had a whole-body smile.

The pools in the front of the park were bathing suit required and occupied by yelling children and a few loud beer drinking adults. In the center of the park were three pools: one hot, one super-hot and one cool, fenced in near our cabin. The sign on the fence announced no clothing allowed. In the price of the room was also included a one hour stay in a private hot springs bath which was fenced in and open to the starry sky. It could easily have accommodated five people without touching. I spent an hour floating, arms spread out and communed with the stars while pondering the whole New Orleans experience. I also spent hours in the no-clothing tubs and had all three to myself most of the time that evening and the next morning. I spent time in silent meditation receiving guidance and healing resulting in the releases of my past life experiences. I felt the joy of release.

Angels worked with me and they felt so tangibly present, stimulating tingles all over. This beautiful energy heightened the experience of the hot springs water and the energies of this place. Chakra imbalances that had carried forward from the slave lifetime into this lifetime were being healed. The main one was dislocation of my first chakra, made to protect myself during the slave lifetime. Midway during my soak, a thirty something woman opened the gate

23

and stopped immediately. I looked up briefly from my float in the hot pool to see her standing in the large wooden door.

"Oh, my alone time is over," I thought and went back into the deep healing meditation anyway. A short time later, I heard the gate gently close, which was a feat considering the type and size of the gate. Looking up again a little later, she was not there. I believe she decided not to interrupt my meditations and left quietly. I was relieved and grateful for her sensitivity and generosity of spirit. No one else entered the entire evening and in the morning, I again had these pools to myself. The checkout time was generous and I used every minute of it. It was a beautiful experience! I held it in my heart with deep and wide gratitude and so much joy. It was so freeing going across the country. I was the only constant in a sea of new experiences. I felt unbridled joy for a time, feeling free to do as I wanted along the way. Stopping when I wanted, going when I felt the urge to keep heading West to whatever was waiting for me there. Whatever it was, it would be new and different. Perhaps I had become too comfortable in my routine in North Carolina. I had been cruising and not growing. It was time to go and time to grow. This brought a smile to my face. I pet Ms. Carley and she smiled too.

Chapter Five
Doggone It

Now I was driving swiftly on the last leg of my journey from Faywood to Phoenix, AZ.

"Hi hon, how are you?"

"Good, and you?" responded Marc.

"Well, I'm in a geological anomaly that I've never seen anywhere and didn't expect in this desert terrain. There are large standing boulders everywhere. It's full of rocks that look like some giants played a game throwing them around or an ancient volcano spewed them out.

"Oh, that's Texas Canyon."

"It's pretty unique."

"That it is and that's exciting because it means I'll see you tonight, right?

"That's my plan. I've talked with Val and she's going to be home when I get there. She's excited too."

"Well, I'll see you over there tonight."

"I'll let you know when I've landed. Maybe we could all go to dinner together."

"Sounds good. Love you."

"Love you too."

On the drive from Texas Canyon, the number of Sahuaro cacti increased steadily. Few trees existed in this desert terrain. I remember Marc's friend taking me to Sahuaro National Monument. He kept asking,

"Isn't it beautiful?" over and over again. Finally, I responded,

"It's another friggen Sahuaro," he too seemed disappointed at my lack of enthusiasm for the desert.

The drive to Phoenix was smooth and uneventful until I arrived at Scottsdale.

*****

Valorie's excited wave welcomed me. As she neared the car her face fell from smile to frown.

"Hi, what's wrong?"

"Oh, I had no idea Carley was a border collie mix. My Patches does not like this type of dog. She's a rescue, and I think she was attacked by a border collie. I have to watch where I walk her and make sure no border collie types are around."

"Oh no. That could be a problem. Can we try and see how they react outside?"

I put Carley on a leash and Val went to get Patches also on a leash. As soon as Patches saw Carley she went berserk. She barked, growled and lunged at Carley. It took all of Val's strength to keep them apart. I put Carley back in the car and Patches still reacted strongly. While Val took Patches inside, I called an animal communicator, who informed us that Patches would fight Carley to the death. She said something about past lives and that Patches would not be calmed. She recommended it would not be safe to have them in the same space at all. Val and I asked our guidance and we both got confirmation; we agreed staying with her was not an option.

"Marc, hi."

"Are you here yet?

"Yes, I'm in Scottsdale at Val's and we have a problem."

"What kind of problem, can I help?"

"Val's dog, Patches, will not tolerate Carley. Patches has a problem with border collie breeds and she tried to attack Carley. I don't know what to do. I can't stay at Val's with Carley." I related the animal communicator's take on it and the results of our own meditations.

After a pause, Marc said,

"Come move in with me. You are both welcome. It's small but we can work it out - I'm sure."

"Are you sure? This is quite an imposition." After another short pause, he said definitively,

"I'm sure," and he related the directions to get to his one-bedroom apartment in Mesa in the Phoenix Valley.

This would be one way to find out if we were compatible in a hurry. I imagined Marc straightening up and trying to figure out how we were going to manage while we found our way to his apartment complex which housed mainly students of the nearby Maricopa Community College. We were in the bottom floor which was part above and part below ground which provided welcome cool in the desert.

* * * * *

I had already purchased a basic kitchen for Marc when I visited in December for his birthday. Back then I had asked him,

"What is your favorite meal?"

This is a question most people would answer with one or two if not three or four options. Marc couldn't think of what his favorite meal was!!! It took quite a bit of time for him to say,

"I think it would be a nice steak with green beans and mashed potatoes with lots of butter and chocolate mousse for dessert. Is that OK?"

"If that's what you want, that's what you'll get." I replied with confidence.

After Marc went to work that day, I looked in his kitchen and found the following inventory: one small sauce pan with no lid, a sad frying pan, two forks, three knives, four spoons, two cups, two plates, two glasses, paper plates, one roll of aluminum foil.

"How does anyone cook anything besides TV dinners in this kitchen?" I asked the walls. Later I learned it was adequate for spaghetti noodles with butter no sauce and eggs which is what he lived on aside from occasional dinners out.

A trip to the mall later, he had a basic but complete kitchen in which I could prepare his birthday dinner. In retrospect, it would have been way cheaper to take him out for dinner! After setting the chocolate mousse into the fridge, Valorie took me shopping with her. I had planned a candle lit bath for him as well.

"So those sparkles I saw between you two in October were real. He seems like such a nice guy."

"I agree. Well, I'm sorry I didn't answer when you asked if there was something between us. I just wasn't ready to talk about it. It happened so suddenly and unexpectedly."

"Yes, now that you've told me the story, it was a big surprise in Surprise," we both had a good laugh. It seems I was forgiven for not talking with her about it.

I picked up one candle, then put it back. Looked around, picked up several others just to put them back again.

"I've never seen anyone spend so much time deciding on candles!"

Maybe I was obsessing a bit and maybe more than a bit. It wasn't really about the candles; I was nervous about this whole thing and wanted this day to be perfect. I still didn't know how things would develop between us. What I didn't know was that Marc was a man of simple tastes. I am a creature of comforts. He barely knew any. His apartment was as spartan as a monk's quarters.

After greeting Marc at the door, I led him to the candle-lit bathroom. His broad, slightly uncomfortable smile was reward enough for all the preparations. I turned on the hot water in the mostly drawn bubble bath, instructing him to get it to his preferred temperature and left him to soak while I competed the dinner preparations.

Marc ate happily but was not effusive about the dinner. It was clear he was not a "foodie." We had so much to talk about, so much history to catch up on. Time flew by as we traded stories comfortably. Marc attended the Peabody Conservatory for music and was chosen to do an exceedingly difficult Russian piano piece for his final high school concert, orchestra and all. He had to choose between continuing to study piano and music composition or going to MIT in engineering. Sitting in a small room playing piano 8 hours a day and the small market for professional piano players led him to a decision to go to MIT, plus this would get him further from home, an important criterion for a teenager.

Marc shared some of his early metaphysical experiences. The one that sticks out in my mind is his first Communion, an unusual memory for a person raised in a Jewish household.

I told Marc the story of my near-death experience backpacking in the wilderness of WV[2] and how I went to graduate school on $12.50.

"You do seem to have a knack for following your guidance," Marc said after considering the story. "Is it easy for you?"

"Not always. Some people think I'm courageous, but I think I may be more afraid of boredom than I am of the adventure of following guidance. The near-death experience certainly propelled me forward, but we all have things that do that for us. You, for example, recently left a 28-year marriage. That took a lot of courage, and I'm sure there were signal moments that led to the decision. It's not one you made lightly."

"Agreed; I had reached the point where, as far as I could tell, the alternative was worse. I could see my marriage getting more and more dysfunctional, affecting the whole family in negative ways. I didn't want us turning into Frank and Marie Barrone from *Everybody Loves Raymond*. At least this way, by separating, there was hope we would each find new inspiration on how to live our lives, for my ex, my son and myself."

"Everyone has to decide for him/herself when it is time to change. I think we both knew when it was the right time for us."

I brought out the Crystal Ally Cards and gave Marc a reading as part of his birthday gift.

---

[2] For the full Near-Death Story see **Thirsting for a Raindrop** Chapter 2: Otter Creek Wilderness

"Those are very helpful cards," observed Marc at the close of the reading.

"I'm glad you like them. Let's dance," I invited as I put on some nice slow music and extended my hand. Marc hesitated, then rose and started to dance. This is when I discovered that despite his extensive musical background, his ability to keep time perfectly when he played guitar and piano did not seem to penetrate to his feet. We swayed a bit and hugged and laughed. It was sweet. Fancy or not, I realized dancing also brings me joy.

Chapter Six
Doing Desert

Settling into the apartment, we rearranged things to give us each some private space. Since neither of us had many things, it did not take long. We turned the living room into another bedroom. I made dinner in the now better stocked kitchen by adding some of my favorite items I managed to fit into the car. In the morning after breakfast, Marc left for work. I started trying to find my way around town.

"Where am I now?" I wondered, feeling disoriented yet again.

I called Marc, who had not yet tired of being my personal GPS, for the second time that day getting directions to his apartment when it should have been natural for me. Phoenix was developed by a bunch of Midwesterners and they planned it to be a rectangular grid like Chicago where I grew up. The angled street exceptions were named the same as the ones in Chicago. But every day I found myself disoriented, turned around and downright dizzy.

Finally, home again, I sat in meditation asking,

"Why am I here? Why am I so disoriented?"

I sat a long time in silence feeling a greater and greater connection to the quantum field/zero point. Slowly, I started to get the idea that I was supposed to do some energy healing work around this area. I was shown a picture of two energy vortices. They looked like large funnels with their point at the earth's surface and the open end in the sky. I noticed they were moving in different directions.

* * * * *

In Sedona with Valorie during my first trip, I had encountered some energy vortices where energy gathers into a vortex shape and moves clockwise or counterclockwise. I had been quite skeptical of the idea of vortices until I climbed Cathedral Rock where my hair stood up on my entire body with the strong energy. Something real was there. I felt tingles all over for hours after that climb and on my way down, a tall buff young black man with bleached blonde hair came directly toward me as if he knew me, stopped in front of me, placed one hand on his slung hip, lifted the other with a flip and loudly asked,

"Honey, what's up with all this vortex business?" He swept the landscape with his free arm, leaned forward in a challenge and waited. In response, I stepped a little closer so I could put my buzzing hands up to his ears. He closed his eyes and felt the energy as indicated by the 'ooooooo' formed on his mouth and the raise of his well-groomed eyebrows and said,

"OK now, I'm going, I'm going, OK now, that's it," he turned around and glided toward the path to the top of the rocks.

"Alright now, there is something to this," I heard him say as he rejoined his group.

Later that day we spent an afternoon playing in Oak Creek and a heron landed on the red rocks directly across from us. The heron stayed there the whole time we played in the water.

"What joy this is!" I exclaimed to Valorie.

"Yes, simple pleasures," said Val with a broad satisfied smile.

* * * * *

The next day in Phoenix in meditation, I was guided to drive to a particular park area. Once there, I started walking and saw a large Mormon temple. I was led to a bench and guided to sit. A vision of two large vortices appeared like the ones I had been shown the previous day. I was told they were rotating in the wrong directions, then got the impression I was to correct this.

"*How do I do this?*" I asked.

"With your intention and your well-earned will forces. Intend them to rotate in the right direction."

An image of the right direction appeared and I thought with my strength of will,

"Reverse direction now at a rate that is easy to tolerate." I imagined them turning the right way while watching with my inner sight as the vortices responded to my will. As they reversed direction, the fog in my head started to clear. Then the dizziness dissipated and I no longer felt disoriented.

For the first time, I needed no help finding my way back to the apartment! I felt a flood of joy rush through me as I allowed it to sink in that I had just righted two vortices the size of large high-rise apartment buildings and shifted the energy in the area. What a trip! I didn't need to know how or even what, I just needed to be open to guidance and to ask questions and I learned so much in the process. I started reading books on earth energy lines and learned large buildings and especially those with peaked towers, like churches, are either built on ley lines or can shift ley lines by their presence. My friend, Joseph Asterita, was also studying this area and we had interesting conversations about earth healing work.

Could this be why I was sent to Arizona? I felt something inside that I had not felt since arriving here. What was that? After some soul searching, I realized I finally felt something I never expected: joy at being here in the desert!

Chapter Seven
Gems and Minerals and Fossils, Oh My!

The main reason I left North Carolina when I did was to get to Arizona in time to go to the famous Tucson Gem and Mineral Show, the largest of its kind in the world. Having a store called The Sacred Stone Center, I was most interested in attending and buying. I still had the store in my office back in North Carolina with another healer using the office and selling stones for me. It was a small operation and one we both enjoyed.

The entire city of Tucson turns into a show for this event. The only one larger is the Paris Air Show. Every motel was full of rooms with beds against the walls to allow sales tables full of glimmering, beautiful, powerful stones.

Starr Pass Road was where the metaphysical stone people gathered. All spaces inside and outside the motel had been turned into stores. The lobby was full of beautiful stones and rutilated vogels from Brazil which became one of my first purchases. Taking them back to the car, I could feel the energy was overwhelming. I put tourmalines in my pockets to better ground me, and connected in with the heart of Gaia, Earth Mother before I felt I could begin to walk again. I went back into the motel when I felt centered. I found my favorite vendor, Heaven and Earth Jewelry. I wanted to buy everything, but knew I had a budget to stick to. I purchased a few things and listened to Robert Simmons talk about new discoveries. I stayed away from the Moldavite because it lifted me out of my body. Robert's wife wore a magnificent clear green Moldavite that looked like a 12 Carat emerald and I had to limit the amount of time I talked with her.

Outside for some air I started to explore the sea of tents and tables behind the motel.

"Hallllllllp." I heard a faint call.

"*Who needs help?*" I asked internally.

"*Hallllllllllp,*" the call continued and I followed the impulse through many tables and tents. Eventually I stood at an uncovered card table in the center of the sea and saw a beautiful quartz crystal shaped in a way that invited you to hold it to your heart. It was about 9 inches tall, flat on the bottom. Smaller at the bottom, it curved up in a pleasing way to the widest part, then curved back to a point at the top. It had beautiful white inclusions one looked like an angel. It was traumatized and when I held it, I got the impression someone, likely the person selling it, had used it for some dark negative purpose.

"How much?" I asked still holding the stone. He quoted a price too high for this stone and I asked if I could get a discount since I was a wholesaler.

"The price is the price lady," he said strongly. "Cash only."

Well, I had some cash. The other stones on the table were also sad and suffering. I bought as many as I could afford and took them to the car. I did an initial clearing for them, went for lunch and started my search again. It took me months to clear those stones. Once cleared the original stone became an altar piece for Julianah.

I had not always been able to hear crystals. A pair of women came into my life a few years earlier and initiated me as a crystal keeper and opened my perceptions to the kingdom of stones. Sometimes we have to seek out trainings and attunements and sometimes they come and find us. The trick is to recognize them and seize the opportunities when they arise even if it doesn't seem practical or reasonable. It only has to be right.

I tried to walk in front of a celestial crystal that probably weighed in at 600 lbs. Its energy was so forceful I had to back up and walk around its non-pointed side. Then an amethyst geode 12 feet high, four to five feet wide in a kind of figure 8 called to me. I loved it and put it on my list of things to acquire in case of a lottery win. So much beauty, so much energy! I bought a few other crystals I was sure would sell and called it a day. I had to drink double the water I usually did in the desert which was double what I drank in humid climates. It also made me hungrier than usual. I ate one more meal and then headed home exhausted. Crystals often brought joy but sorting through them and finding the right ones in an overwhelming atmosphere I found taxing.

Maybe I needed to adjust my attitude I mused on my way to sleep that night. This should be a joyful endeavor.

"*How do I do that?*" I asked and fell into a deep sleep.

In the morning I had a dream about putting out a strong field of love to cushion the energies at the show. I felt more relaxed knowing I would find the stones that were for me to purchase. After all, I had already responded to some stones that needed to be rescued out of an ocean of crystal vendors.

"Slow down, t*rust, relax and enjoy,*" were the words that occurred.

"*Trust, relax and enjoy the process and this will bring greater joy. Focus on the positive and let go of the rest. You don't have to be perfect; you already are.*"

That worked.

One day I got off at the exit before Starr Pass thinking it was my exit. All the vendors here specialized in fossils and I did not collect them. I parked where I was guided and asked,

"*Why am I here?*"

I felt an urge to go into the store in front of me and walked directly to a golden calcite stalactite two and a half feet tall weighing around 25 pounds. I learned it was from China. I had been given an assignment to work on the ascension grid over China and I got the impression it was to be used to focus energy there. I negotiated a good price for it and carried it to the trunk. Seems it was not a mistake to get off at this exit after all. I felt gratitude and gratitude brings joy on its coattails.

Chapter Eight
Cool, Clear, Water

A few weeks after Tucson, I realized what I loved about the desert was being able to wear sandals every day even in January and February. But I craved water. I had been taking long showers and baths, sometimes twice a day, but that was not enough. I yearned for water. I was accustomed to having a floating experience in water regularly in warm seasons. Summers we spent across the street from a lovely little lake in Wisconsin and I swam every day there wasn't lightning, Everywhere I had lived I had rivers or lakes or pools or ocean or all the above to access regularly. I had learned the drive to Pleasant Lake here, the closest large body of water and Carley loved to go there but that was too long a drive to do every day.

"I need a daily dose of outdoor water that's close by," I confessed to Marc that night.

"Try Dobson Ranch, it was built before water conservation was put in place here in the Phoenix Valley. The irrigation canals run through the neighborhood, but it's private property. Don't know if you can walk there."

"We'll see." I said hooking Carley up to her collar. We headed off to the ranch which was a housing development just about a mile from the apartment. Carley walked next to the water-filled canal on red brick colored smooth walking paths lined with lovely flowering bushes to the left. Friendly smiles nodded hello. Bicyclers zipped past in their lane and many dogs passed by with their owners in tow. I loved being by the water and it became our daily walk.

"Someone is going to stop you, you are supposed to be a resident," said Marc.

"We'll see," said I, not nearly as bothered by regulations. I began a daily routine of walking at the canals.

One day while walking Carley, a man on a bike next to an official looking truck moved his bicycle across in front of me to block my way. I stopped and said hello. I thought,

"Well, maybe my time is up here. Maybe Marc is right, they're going to stop me walking here because I'm not a resident. OK, it's been a good run."

"Hi, how's it going?" opened the man on the bike.

"Really well, and you?"

"Great, thank you." What's your dog's name?"

They were very chatty and told me of their long running relationship to the ranch and the canals. The man with the truck had been working on this canal since the very beginning. He was probably 20 years older than me and the one on the bike was five to ten years younger.

"I've worked here since she was built," said the man with the truck with pride. "I'm the one that keeps things going."

"I've been his friend for years now," added the man with the bike. "I help him out when I can. Where are you from?"

I was careful not to mention I didn't live in the subdivision as I explained my recent transition to the desert of Arizona. They both offered their names and kept asking questions. We chatted amiably for a time and it became clear that both of them were flirting with me. I chuckled inside feeling flattered and tickled.

"See you tomorrow?" asked the bicycle man.

"God willing and the creek don't rise," I joked.

"No chance of the creek rising this time of year," was the response from the man with the truck. I laughed out loud when I returned to the car and when I related the story to Marc, I concluded,

"So, I don't think you have to worry about me getting kicked off the property."

"No, but I may have other worries now," he smiled. Marc claimed not to be a jealous man and his smile and energy indicated that was the case.

The next major find was a place called Tonopah: a hot mineral springs oasis, a 45-minute drive from Phoenix in good traffic. When I first went there, it was a nudist camp which didn't bother me. I preferred being free of a plastic bathing suit in hot mineral springs. The camp was rustic and had various hot tubs - some manufactured, some made of stone, some enclosed and others open to the desert. All rather funky and fun. Each bath had a name. If you wanted, you could have a completely enclosed private tub. I preferred one on the back of the property open to the surrounding desert where I could watch the sunset. The streams that ran between tubs had bamboo and many birds including blackbirds. It was truly an oasis. It was a place to renew and refresh body, mind and spirit. I joined immediately obtaining a frequent soaker card covering ten baths at a discount as I knew I would be back frequently. It was an inexpensive vacation from the dryness of Phoenix and not too long a drive for the pleasure of this kind of soak. It was also a place where I could write and meditate deeply.

* * * * *

Marc invited me to go out to eat one day and when he came home from work he asked,

"What kind of restaurant do you want tonight?"

"I want Chinese. I want a place where mostly Chinese people go, one that has lazy-susans in the middle of the table, great food at a great price. Marc was learning how to muscle test for right answers. I was working on using my intuition more of the time.

"I don't know such a place," commented Marc after a short consideration.

"I'll drive," I offered.

I asked inside if there was this type of place and got an intuitive yes. I asked Marc to muscle test for confirmation and he got a solid yes. Open to guidance, I felt the highway was the place to start. I followed directions as I heard them: *"get on here, exit here, turn right, go three lights and turn left.*" I did so and we ended up in a parking lot for a Mexican restaurant.

"Maybe I heard wrong?"

"No, I get that we are in the right place," he confirmed.

"*Back up.*" came into my head. When I did, there behind us was Wong's Place. We entered to 80% Chinese customers, the tables even had lazy-susans and it smelled great.

"Well, maybe it did work."

"Apparently," mused Marc a little surprised.

The food was fresh, tasty and well prepared. The bill was more than reasonable. We returned frequently as it became one of our favorite places to eat out. It was a joy having a partner who was willing to align with Divine Will and listen to guidance.

When the temperature hit 110, I wondered,

"How long would I have to stay in the desert? Jesus only had to go for forty days and forty nights, it seems to me, I've already been here longer than that.

Chapter Nine
Two AM

"What do you want me to do?" I asked internally. It was 2:00 o'clock in the morning. I was wide awake; it was the kind of awake that indicated there was no going back to sleep, so in the meditation chair I asked again,

"What do you want me to do?" and sat in silence centering myself and aligning with Divine Source despite my slightly disgruntled temper at being awakened. I like my sleep and I like it in one long continuous stretch. I have rarely been a nap person.

A vision of a man on an airplane came to me. He was terrified and embarrassed that he was terrified. He was hugging a pillow pretending to be asleep but he was shaking. Not a person I recognized but I could feel his pain.

"Pray for him and send him peaceful energy," was the direction I received. It was more a feeling than words. I asked for angels to bring him peace. I spent about an hour sending him peace from my heart and it looked like he fell asleep. So sweet. Forgetting the hour, I was happy to help. I felt joy. Then, I realized what time it was and wondered if I could sleep now. I went back to bed and fell asleep quickly.

In the morning I got up at usual time and midafternoon I realized I didn't feel any lack of sleep. I didn't have a regular schedule yet here in Arizona, but I tried to keep the same hours Marc did, so I would not disturb him despite my proclivity for being a night owl. Being a morning person, he worked early hours to avoid traffic.

Many mornings I was awakened between 2:00 and 4:00 AM and I generally asked what they wanted me to do and got an answer and followed the directions and never missed the sleep which, for me, was amazing.

I went back to bed for a few hours and woke amid a dream. I was walking through the desert and the vista before me was a dull black and white. I was guided to turn around and everything behind me was colorful and bright. I wondered,

"*What does this mean?*" No immediate answer came in and I pondered this a long time. Later, I came to believe that it meant I was to learn to appreciate the unique beauty of the desert. I wondered how long that would take.

Chapter Ten
Cocaine

As I was learning my way around the area, I was guided to many places to do healing work. I spent time daily in mediation much of which was listening to what I was to do: Earth Healing. Some of my friends say this is a misnomer and it may be. The Earth doesn't need healing exactly. Mother Earth will correct our errors one way or another. So technically, what we are healing are the misalignments of energies due to the human interventions which are not for the highest good of all.

During the week while Marc was at work I went around Metropolitan Phoenix (known as the Valley of the Sun) following directions for righting energies. On weekends, Marc, being a Sagittarius, loved to travel.
One week I asked,
"Can we make it to Bluff, Utah in a weekend?"
"Let me check," after consulting maps and the internet, he said,
"Sure. What's in Bluff? It's near Four Corners but there's not much out there."
"I'm reading a book by Virginia Essene, *The Earth, the Cosmos and You: Revelations by Archangel Michael*. She says Archangel Michael has put down his Sword of Light in Bluff, Utah and declared that it will be the first place to ascend into fifth dimension on this continent. I would like to experience this place. I feel a pull to go."
"Sounds interesting. Dan's outfit has a concert this weekend I want to attend and you are welcome to come but the next weekend is clear to go."
"Sounds good."

* * * * *

JJ Cale, author of the songs *Cocaine* and *After Midnight*, walked onto stage, sat on a stool, arm resting on his guitar, looked around for a long time as if he were sizing up the crowd before he started to talk to us in a conversational tone. The theater held about 200 and it was a little more than half full. His laid-back approach was charming and I enjoyed his performances familiar and new to me.

During the intermission I stood in a circle of people including Abby, the wife of the producer. I had met her briefly once before and the introduction had not been friendly. She was a reflexologist so I thought we would have some things in common to talk about but our conversation was flat.

"Oh, I want to introduce Carlos, another of our musicians," she went on and on about his qualifications and how excited they were to have him on board. He was a good looking Peruvian and his concert would be soon. He seemed slightly embarrassed by the effusive introduction. Abby went around the circle introducing various people with brief descriptions of who they were or what they did. Marc had gone to the bathroom. When she came to me, she made several rude comments. I was shocked, flushed with embarrassment and anger. With less self-control there would have been a bitchfight right then and there. I excused myself, went to the bathroom to regain my center and to avoid saying the smart-assed, vindictive answers galloping through my mind. I felt mortified and unfairly judged.

I waited until the lights flashed, went back out to my seat next to Marc and was grateful for the shelter of the dark theater. I managed to calm the storm in my belly enough to be able to enjoy the last half of the concert. I wanted to take a higher road. We both stood for an ovation and after the final encore Marc said,

"I need to go talk with some people…"

"No. I need to go and I need to go now." I stated emphatically and headed directly for the exit. The emphatic tone, one Marc had not yet heard from me, prompted him to let go of his schmoozing plans and we went directly to the car. In the car I related the story to Marc and he was shocked as well. After some consideration Marc confided,

46

"Abby was a good friend of my ex-wife's. She is probably having a hard time adjusting to the separation and pending divorce."

"I get that and I get that it seems really quick that we are together. It's certainly quicker than I had anticipated. But there's more to this. My feelings are way deeper and wider than even this situation warrants." I explained. I asked internally if there were past lives involved and got a strong 'yes'.

"I think I have past lives to clear with her. Would you mind holding space while driving or maybe we could just park somewhere else so I can do the clearing while the emotions are so alive."

"Of course! I'd be happy to. I think I can hold space and drive at the same time. Let's try that - if it doesn't work, I'll stop. But I feel you would prefer to leave this area now. Am I right?" I nodded in grateful accord flashing a 'you don't know the extent' look in his direction in the driver's seat of his green Subaru Forester.

I went into meditation, asking permission to enter the Akashic Records. In a short time propelled by the strong emotions, I reported,

"I see a small castle, lots of stone, cold walkways, big doorways, large tapestries. Ladies in long velvet dresses, somewhere in the late 1500's I'd guess. She is my sister and I'm the younger. She is not attractive and she's mean and she runs her suitors off. It reminds me of Shakespeare's *Taming of the Shrew*. I was more attractive and had multiple suitors and one that I was ready to marry." Marc listened while he drove. I could feel his energy holding space making it easier for me to access the records.

"It's been a year now and she is still not married and I am getting to the age that a woman is considered old not to be married. I appealed to our parents and received permission to marry. She considered this a terrible insult and sees no responsibility of her own in creating the situation. I can feel how angry she is. I think she still carries this anger."

"Makes sense," commented Marc.

"I will ask what I right action to heal this lifetime… I hear a rewrite would work. Do you get agreement?"

Marc muscle tested while driving and got confirmation.

In the rewrite, I imagined that I found a man who could fall in love with her and encouraged him to court her. Also encouraging her to be responsive and the two of them fell in love and I saw the wedding.

"It's beautiful, the church is all decked out with white ribbons and flowers and a runner. I am in a small room helping her with her hair and gown. She looks happy and almost pretty. Now it is moving to a later date when she is pregnant and happy and it was now my turn to get married."

The rewrite felt complete and I felt relieved. I was grateful and ended with my clearing. Marc agreed that the energy shift was significant. I slept way better that night as a result.

Two weekends later we were invited to a barbecue at their house. Many different people were there, a few I recognized from the concert. Abby came up to me, greeted me warmly and thanked me for coming. To my surprise, it felt sincere. She brought me around the room introducing me to various people in a polite way. We had a conversation about how the dry air of Phoenix affects your hair and she suggested I get a perm like her new one. Hers was a tight-curled perm, something I had hated on me but I appreciated the thought.

Later, I overheard her saying to another guest,

"I don't know what happened with Lyneah but she has changed and seems so nice now. We had a lovely conversation..."

I smiled over my glass of wine. I had neither seen nor talked with her since the concert two weeks ago. The only thing that happened between us was the past life clearing and she didn't even know about it. I was grateful that the clearing had affected her in such a positive way but it did not take me to a place of liking her; it just took me to a place where I didn't want to hurt her anymore and that would have to do for now. I didn't want to interfere with Marc's relationship with her and her husband. Marc considered Dan his best friend. I would work to allow our relationship to be based on what happened in the here and now untainted by what had happened a couple hundred years ago or even two weeks ago.

Chapter Eleven
Being

2:00 AM again and I'm wide awake. After completing my mid-sleep nature call, I headed to the meditation chair knowing there would be no sleep until I answered this spiritual call.

Sitting upright, I slipped easily now into meditation. Rudolph Steiner says that in meditation if you want to bring in the higher spiritual energies you should sit upright; having your spine erect helps with this process. If you want to tie into the emotional aspects of your soul, lying down facilitates that. This is helpful in past life clearings, for we follow the threads of the emotions into the Akashic Records to discover their origin.

This had become a nightly routine at least 5 days a week rising between 2 and 4 AM for about two hours. I had started to enjoy this because at that time of day there is a stillness both on the physical and psychic levels. It's like that in airplanes; above the din of everyday thoughts, feelings conversations, TV and radio waves you can find a special stillness.

This morning as I slipped into a meditative state I asked, "*What do you want me to do?*"

There was no answer. I waited and asked again,

"*What do you want me to do?*" I paused and repeated this several times.

Still no answer. I was feeling frustrated.

"*You friggen got me up at 2 AM and I would like to know what you want?*"

"*Be the peace,*" came the answer. I realized the first question was not big enough. It was not about doing it was about being. Sometimes we need to look at the question.

Another night the answer,

"*Be the joy.*" came clearly and quickly because now I had the right question.

"*How do I do that?*"

A tableau of memories came through my mind, all of them ones that created great joy for me. Next, I saw an image of the energy of joy followed by an image of my heart radiating these energies. OK, now I had the how, the next question was,

"*Why?*"

"*There is a balance in the world between the positive and the negative energies. Currently there are not enough people conscious being joyful and your being joyful will contribute to a healthier balance for the world.*"

I started learning how to create joy in my heart by remembering circumstances that brought me great joy: seeing my newborn daughter's face for the first time, swimming with dolphins, great parties, helping a friend, laughing with friends, times when Spirit provided something so small it astounded me that I was worth the attention. After a time, I started thinking of joyous movie scenes which helped pass the time in a fun way (thank you Billy Crystal, Meg Ryan and *What's New Pussycat*).

As I spent more and more nights in this meditation, I started thinking about things that I would like to bring into my life that would start a flow of joy and this felt like a creative way of spending these two hours of meditation. It became fun and the joyous energy gave a welcome lift to my spirit. I performed this meditation many nights as guided, and eventually got to the place where I could sit in the energy of joy in a very pure way without any visuals or memories to stimulate this energy. I know actors and singers practice this to have various emotions readily available on call.

The interesting thing is I never missed the sleep. I woke more refreshed on mornings after meditation than on nights I slept through. It is not that I did not meditate during the day, I usually did for at least one hour. It's just that I was available, not yet having regular work, to help with this pool of meditators. I was not alone. I could feel there were others around the world meditating in a similar way. I felt connected. I felt I was contributing in an important way which led to even brighter joy.

One night I got an image of me doing the joy meditation standing in line at the grocery store.

"*Good idea,*" I thought. "*Anytime you have to wait, just do this meditation and it makes waiting fun.*"

Next, I saw myself teaching a class in a different living room with a fireplace and parquet floors. I was teaching people to meditate creating the energy of joy. I think this could work for anyone. Why don't you try it and see if it would work for you?

* * * * *

In summer, I had to wear gloves to open my car door because it was too hot to touch! I should have invested in moisturizer stocks. I went through two to three times the moisturizer I was accustomed to using.

"Marc I am so tired of this relentless heat; can we please go to San Diego this weekend?"

"I don't see why not."

"Great, I'll make arrangements for a place to stay. Let's leave early Saturday and come back Sunday."

San Diego is known for having wonderful weather year-round. It was in the low 80's and people were complaining about how hot it was. It was 112 when we left Phoenix and I wanted to tell them to shut up!!! Marc drove us around the area. He did not want to go to the zoo.

"I don't like the feel of the animals so confined."

I could understand that. Marc drove to the grand Hotel del Coranado, the largest wooden hotel on the West coast. I talked him into parking so I could go in to see the interior.

"The ocean is calling me and I must go," I said in the afternoon, strongly feeling Marc was resistant to this idea. We returned to the motel, put bathing suits on, grabbed beach towels and headed out. I was delighted and Marc dragged his feet. He observed me lighting up the closer I got to the ocean. I laid the blanket down, took off my beach dress, sprang up and sprinted into the surf so happy to be in the ocean again. I felt so free in the waves. The water was a perfect temperature and I could have stayed all day.

It wasn't much later Marc, still on the blanket, asked if I was ready to go. I was disappointed, I had waited months to get to the ocean and now all I had was an hour to be here? My idea of going to the beach included arriving in the morning, laying in the sun, swimming, laying in the sun, swimming, laying in the sun, going for lunch and then returning to an afternoon of the same. I was used to doing this more like once a month than once a year. Later, he admitted he thought this might be a deal breaker for him when he saw how much I lit up at the beach. He was not comfortable at the ocean and not comfortable admitting the extent of his discomfort. His very fair skin burned easily and he did not float but there was more.

"You really lit up," Marc later remarked.

"The ocean does that for me. I feel so refreshed and renewed after a swim."

Since he looked rather morose, I asked,

"Have you looked into your past lives near the ocean?" Images appeared before my eyes as he spoke.

"Not yet," he said reluctantly.

"Well, when you are ready, we can work on clearing them."

Chapter Twelve
Teec Nos Pos

"Let's leave for Bluff Friday night as soon as I can get home from work so we get a good start on the weekend. We should take some food and drink with us because there won't be much along the way for most of the trip. It's not like the East Coast; there can be hours without even a gas station. A lot of what we'll go through will be reservation land."

"Is it all desert?"

"Well, mostly, but different kinds of deserts and some red rock country which has its own beauty. Some of it is ranch cattle land, some horse country all of it is mostly Mormon or Navajo. Bluff is in red rocks territory. There is likely to be no cell phone service much of the time and we have to know where to gas up." This sounded so different from what I was accustomed to on the East Coast, where it was rare to go even a half hour without any signs of civilization. I was so intrigued that I forgot to ask how long it would take.

*****

We left after the rush, drove until dark and found a basic motel at Flagstaff, stayed the night, rose early and headed out after a good breakfast. Miles and miles without phone coverage and wide-open spaces.

"Well, there's no chance we will run out of scenery for cowboy movies," I exclaimed after hours of driving. We stopped occasionally and everyone we encountered was somber, Mormon and Navajo alike. In the car, we talked easily and traveled in silence equally well but the landscape was anything but comfortable. 'Teec Nos Pos' announced the sign for the trading post, which was a welcome sign of commerce. We learned it was pronounced "Teesnospos." Stretching our legs and looking at the beautiful handmade artwork, I noticed Marc talking with another non-native man.

"I used to live in Farmington, New Mexico," I heard him say.

"You wouldn't happen to know Arthur Hartz, would you?" asked Marc.

"My God it's a small world, he was my neighbor…"

Here, as close to the middle of nowhere as I've experienced, Marc found a neighbor of one of his cousins!!!!! He had married a Navajo woman and was living on the reservation. They laughed and engaged in conversation for some time. I was glad for the time to stretch my legs and move around to regain circulation.

I roamed through the rooms in the trading post, larger than it first appeared, looking to see if anything called to me but left empty handed. I was conserving funds, living mostly on savings not having found employment options yet. Marc, however, bought a lovely hand-woven wall hanging. A Native version of the Tree of Life sized to fit a small apartment, compact enough to roll and take along in a move, it was an excellent choice and beautiful. It was Marc's color pallet - earth tones with greens.

We got to Four Corners at a few minutes to five. The Monument is on Navajo land and is the only place in the US where four states come together. You can put your feet in Arizona, New Mexico, Colorado and Utah in a matter of seconds. As we were pulling up, an older Navajo man dressed in a kind of park uniform was locking the gate. We looked disappointed but he guiltlessly pointed to the sign displaying the park hours. We would have to put our feet in several states at once the next day.

As we drove toward Bluff, I felt a shift in energy. I mentioned to Marc that the Vortex started even before we entered the town. I felt happiness there. We checked into our motel which was not much more than a modular basic, but it felt good. The young Native lady who was at the desk was pleasant and smiled broadly. She was fun to talk with, a sharp contrast to everyone else we had encountered in 250 miles today.

"If you could have anything you wanted for dinner, what would that be?" asked Marc.

"Vegetable Pad Thai would be my first choice," I replied thinking that dish would be at least a day's drive from here.

At the Twin Rocks Trading Post and Restaurant next to two towers of red rock, we were surprised again, this time with Pad Thai: shrimp, chicken or vegetarian and it was delicious.

Everyone in the restaurant was also happy and nice. After dinner we walked to the jewelry store. The Heard Museum in Phoenix does not have pieces as beautiful as some in this store. A tall handsome dignified native man stood behind the counter watching us. He had nodded but did not give any indication of being as friendly as the others we had met in this town so far. A stunning Squash Blossom Necklace in exquisite silver work with some of the deepest purple sugilite I'd ever seen called to me. I knew it was way out of my budget but wanted to admire the workmanship closer. He came over and brought the piece onto a velvet pad. It had thirteen good sized pieces of sugilite set in squash blossom silver settings, all hand made. Each one was perfectly created and all were balanced making the piece elegant instead of overstated. I examined it finding no irregularities anywhere in the piece. There were none. It was some of the best silver work I'd ever seen.

"It's exquisite," I commented still admiring the quality of the piece.

"How much?" I asked.

"It is $5,960."

"Wow, that's way out of my budget, but it's worth every penny. Whoever made this is so talented. I have rarely seen silver work so perfect."

He shifted his stance and looked at me in a new way.

"That's different. Most people say it's not worth it."

"Oh, they probably have no idea what it takes to do such work. This is high quality silver work and the pieces of sugilite are unique and so well chosen. If it were in my budget, it would be mine."

His produced a beautiful smile that lit up his face, replaced the large necklace reverently, went over to another case and produced a single pendant with the same deep purple sugilite set in a feather motif silver setting hand made by the same artist.

"Oh, it's wonderful! How much is this one?"

"Forty-five dollars."

With a big smile I said with joy,

"Sold!" It was not only a wonderful reminder of this trip, it also held the vibration of Bluff which is a sweet energy unique to the region. I left the store reluctantly thinking, "*In case of a lottery win the princess turquoise bracelet, the squash blossom necklace and several other pieces will be mine.*"

We slept very peacefully that night and the next day we drove a different way home. On the Native land we saw a few horses, a small single-wide trailer and several miles of uninhabited grass lands. The next place, about five miles down the road, would be one or two single-wides, a cow and a horse, and this repeated over and over until we reached the border of Arizona. No longer reservation land, the terrain changed and it became non-Native ranch land. It was over-grazed, with large herds of cattle occupying little space. The land was dusty and thirsty.

The White Mountains dotted the horizon and we continued to a town I remember because of its name: Show Low. It is a largely Mormon town that was won during an extensive poker game between equal partners in a one-million-acre ranch. They determined there was not enough room for both of them (I wonder what was up with that?). They agreed to settle over a game of "Seven Up" with the winner taking the entire ranch. The game was a marathon and finally to end it Clark said, "If you can show low, you win." In response Cooley turned up the deuce of clubs, the lowest possible card in the deck. The main street is now called Deuce of Clubs.

It was a long ride. I was so tired of sitting by the time we made it back to Phoenix I had trouble getting out of the car. My idea of a weekend drive is not 18 hours of driving! I learned a Sagittarius can go and go and go stopping only for bathroom and quick food breaks. There's no need to stop to see anything or to stay in one place and enjoy it, driving is the goal. Turning around to see something again is out of the question. My idea of a trip is drive two or three hours, stay the weekend, explore the area and drive back.

It needed to include time in some nice water. I suspected it would take considerable work to find a compromise for our travel styles.

Chapter Thirteen
Mysterious Stone

We were meditating regularly now separately and together and one day I was unable to concentrate, it was like there was static in my brain. I took Carley for a walk and had no problem doing a walking meditation at the ranch. Returning to the partially subterranean apartment, I noticed a beautiful stone just outside. It was a layered rectangular sandstone about two feet high, one foot across and four inches thick. I had never noticed it until now. I found it visually attractive, but it felt odd. Who put it here and why? I found it curious and a little disturbing. I looked around the apartments near-by and there was nothing like it anywhere else, so it was not part of the landscaping. Inside, I was totally unable to reach a meditation state. I waited for Marc to come home not wanting to disturb him at work.

"Hi Marc, did you bring that sandstone here?"

"I was going to ask you the same thing."

"Not me."

"Me either."

"I was not able to concentrate in here today. I was able to meditate on our walk but not in here."

"Do you think the stone has something to do with it?"

"I don't know."

I felt odd energies. I felt uncomfortable, like I was being watched. I felt that was crazy and I felt uncomfortable revealing any of this. I tried to let it go thinking this was imagination but eventually I called a shaman friend and asked his take.

"Take that thing far out in the desert and bury it under at least a foot of sand," he instructed. "It is a listening stone. Someone is eavesdropping and it is not someone who has your highest good at heart. Do it as soon as possible." This was the same Shaman who had helped me with some strange occurrences at my house in Durham and had told me Marc had saved me in a previous lifetime before I knew about the New Orleans story.

"Thank you," I said as I hung up.

I explained this to Marc and was relieved and grateful when he grabbed his keys and a towel to wrap the stone. We set off for the open desert outside the city in silence and found a place that felt right to bury the stone.

The next day I had no trouble meditating. I have no idea where the stone came from, I was happy to have it gone.

That night I noticed Marc had some redness on his neck and arms.

"Oh, that's just the family curse," he explained. He told me of his Uncle who wanted his gravestone to say, 'The itching has finally stopped'. I was concerned but Marc acted like it was just a normal part of life.

A few weeks later I noticed Marc had redness all over. When I commented, he said it was normal for him.

It did not seem normal to me and he seemed to be getting more and more tired. His skin condition kept getting worse. I suggested a variety of natural things I knew of but none of them worked for him, some aggravated his situation. His skin condition got so bad he didn't even want to travel! You know a Sag is bad when he won't travel. Finally, I strongly suggested a doctor. Marc didn't follow through.

"Good morning what do you want to do this weekend?"

"I think I'd like to stay home this weekend," replied Marc in a tired way.

"Are you sure you are not allergic to me?"

We enjoyed a light breakfast and he went back to bed to rest. I went out shopping for dinner and when I came back, he was leaning against the counter in the kitchen.

"Are you OK?"

"Not sure," he replied weakly.

I walked over to him just in time to catch him as he fainted! I was able to get him gently to the floor. When he woke, we went to the

ER. He was released with some cream and a referral to a dermatologist. He was dehydrated and had low blood pressure which may have explained the fainting. An integrative medical doctor provided help for his condition, a rare form of psoriasis according to this doctor who was at least able to give him rather simple things that kept it partially under control. The dryness of the climate did not help. We added a humidifier which offered a small amount of relief. Marc slowly healed from this whole-body condition.

"Are you sure you are not allergic to me?"

"I'm sure. You, you bring me joy and happiness."

"Maybe you are allergic to joy and happiness?"

He gave me a reassuring hug.

"This too shall pass," he tried to comfort my doubts. I was not yet convinced. He had already told me the story of his Jewish Mother's attitude many years ago when he dated another Swedish-German woman seriously. Her response was,

"You can marry her if you want, I just won't be there."

She was no longer with us in third dimension, but her energy still lingered in his history even though he was no longer practicing Judaism. As did my Aunt's even though I was no longer a practicing Lutheran and she had also passed.

Chapter Fourteen
Work Search

I had been looking for work and applied for a massage therapy license. I felt more like a criminal than a medical professional as I went through the process where I had to have my fingerprints taken and criminal background checked. I asked if they did this for their other healthcare workers and they looked at me like I had two heads.

"If you want to work in this state you gotta go through this process," was the flat response.

After I made it through the process and got my license, I started seriously looking for a place to do massage. It turns out the reason there were so many hoops to jump through was because so many massage 'practitioners' were not legitimate. Arizona had only recently gone to licensure to differentiate between prostitutes and legitimate therapists.

It also required too much investment to establish a place of my own. So, I started looking for a legitimate establishment to work in. Every practice would only start me at $10.00 an hour. Massage is way too physically taxing to do for $10 an hour and the hour on the table means at least two to three hours of time in set up, tear down, doing laundry, keeping records, and complying with codes. Then there were the fees you have to pay to keep insurance, which the establishment required but did not cover and the annual licensing and CEU requirements, also not inexpensive. At that rate I would be losing money. I would work in a clerical office first.

Despite guidance not to, I applied at several temp agencies. I'd always kept up on my typing and computer skills. On a bad day I could do a 70-wpm test. On the way to the manpower office, an enormous great blue Heron flew in front of my car, looked me straight in the eye, its wing only inches from the windshield. I hit the brakes hard not to collide with it. What was the great blue Heron doing here in the middle of the desert in a dry river? I was accustomed to seeing them in North Carolina but not here. I consider the Heron one of my totem animals and they usually indicate a message from Spirit. This message felt clear: don't bother applying to Manpower. I applied anyway and it turned out to be a waste of time, nothing ever came of it. It was as if they lost my application. Whenever I called, they had a hard time even finding my records. There was a part of me that was joyful at their ineptness. It meant I didn't have to sit in an office which I found toxic. Fluorescent lights and high levels of EMFs make offices less than comfortable.

Our friend Fonda Joyce had moved to Las Vegas and was having a hard time there. Marc suggested we drive up for a weekend to see her and to experience Vegas. I was surprised to really love Vegas. It's an adult playground. We drove to the Valley of Fire which is an other-worldly vista of pink rocks that has been used for science fiction shows. On the way back, I asked Marc what he wanted to do.

"I'd like to sit on one of these bluffs over Lake Mead and have you guide me with your beautiful voice in a meditation."

I obliged with great joy. I thought back over all the dates I had and knew there was no other who would have made this request especially in the Vegas area.

When we returned to town, we went onto the Strip and Marc showed me how to play the slots. We spent around $20 and came out with $40. Fun and decent entertainment. We explored the pyramid despite Marc's apprehension being in the halls when we had no reservation here. I wanted to experience the inside of a pyramid. No one bothered us. Marc started to relax and have fun. This was the kind of person I had been looking for: intelligent, fun, spiritual, kind and caring. Needed some loosening up and I was ok with helping that process. He was balancing me in other ways. We complemented each other in many areas of our lives and easily fit into an I'll cook, you do dishes pattern. Marc readily admits his culinary skills set is a small one. I can attest that he knows how to make pasta with butter and he can cook eggs. He does know how to eat out. The entire Vegas trip was one of joy and getting to know each other better and liking what I saw.

Chapter Fifteen
Embracing Worthiness and Joy

Marc and I were beginning to work together in meditation and in other ways as well. We did ceremony and earth healing work evenings and weekends. One day I received instructions that were clear: record a meditation CD during ceremony on a specific date at a specific time, in our apartment. Marc was to download music to go with the spoken meditation tracks if he agreed. Turns out the time we were told to do the recording was when planet Venus transited the Sun, an auspicious astrological time for divine feminine energies. Marc agreed to work with me on this project.

We set up the recording system and prepared. I was given no idea of what was supposed to be in the content, just that I would be guided. The ceremony set, sacred space opened, I started speaking as I was guided. The recording of the one-hour meditation in one take without edits was surprising. It flowed smoothly and Marc's music came easily as well. We produced and sold 500 copies the first year. I received phone calls from people thanking me for creating this CD. It is designed to help release unworthiness and embrace worthiness. The CD includes the energies of the Venus transit and has a long meditation track and a short one for quicker access.

We were given instructions for two additional CD's that we created together: Embracing Empowerment and Embracing the Divine Feminine. We would be able to sell them at fairs and in stores around the Valley and as we traveled.

Marc had a gig in Chandler at a small country festival. I drove with him and helped him bring in his gear, set up and sell his CD's. Few people stayed to listen, most walked through and continued to other parts of the fair which was noisy. Dan had booked this for Marc. After the performance, which Marc gave his all despite the major distractions, Dan brought an envelope with a check for him and they had a conversation.

"I'm wanting to know when we can cut a CD," asked Marc.

"I'm not sure. I was wondering if you would be interested in working on a musical CD for meditation," replied Dan.

"That's not really what I'm interested in. I have some ideas for songs…" Dan wasn't listening and said he had to go. I could see Marc was still hopeful for Dan's promotional skills to be applied to his songs but it seemed to me Dan was resistant and too 'kind' to say a direct no. I wondered how this would go. I was now even more deeply grateful he was willing to work with me on the meditation CD's.

We attended various Unity Churches in the Valley and some invited Marc to perform. Some also had us do guided meditations together. This worked well and eventually Marc found a church in central Phoenix which we both liked. Here Marc's alternative music style found an appreciative audience. His music was not exactly what you would hear on the radio. It was intelligent music with interesting and often complex lyrics and deep messages, well composed but certainly not your average pop songs. Marc had a deep desire to be recognized as the artist he was. He had received acknowledgment in Jean Houston's Mystery School experiences but he was looking for a wider audience. I was no authority but it seemed to me if he wanted a wider audience, he would have to create simpler songs.

I felt we were both holding back on feeling the joy that was here for us and I started a conversation,

"How did your family deal with joy and happiness?"

"God forbid that you should be too happy," said Marc with an exaggerated Jewish accent. "My tribe's history has been one of persecution for many thousands of years. Often the persecution came when things were good, so there's a genetic inheritance of fear at things being too good because trouble will follow."

"Wow, I hadn't thought of that. Does it curb your joy?"

"I believe it does. I also suspect that I have some past lives which have taught me the same thing."

"Well, we could work on those and the genetic heritage."

"How can we do that?"

"Soul Integration energy work with the intention of clearing through your genetic and your spiritual histories."

"I would be honored if you could help me with that."

"Gladly. I have my own brand of a governor on joy. My Aunt Hay, short for Harriet, used to take an imaginary pin and come over to me when I was feeling especially good. She would use it to pop an imaginary bubble over my head saying it was to help me keep from getting too big a head. She felt it was dangerous to feel too good and to become 'too full of yourself'. She also stopped me if I laughed hard saying,

"Too much laughter results in tears by the end of the day."

"Wow, different culture but the same sentiment. The message is it's not safe to be joyful," mused Marc.

"Yes and on the other hand we'd sing in church summer camp, 'I've got the joy, joy, joy... down in my heart...' so there were many mixed messages."

"Isn't that the truth."

"The question is how do we free ourselves to allow joy to flow without fear of reprisal or compensatory negatives?" I asked.

"Sounds like that's a path we will have to find together and I'm willing to walk it with you. We can start by not curbing joy in each other which may be harder than we think because it means breaking generational patterns. There's a difference between being egotistical and feeling joy," I observed.

"I agree. Let's set our intention to find more joy and to allow ourselves to enjoy it. I'm not afraid of doing some work on this."

"Sounds like a good place to start."

Marc often quoted phrases and pointed out they were either a good song title or a name for a rock group. He spent much time writing, composing and arranging music.

"Enjoying joy. Think there's a song in that?" I asked.

Chapter Sixteen
The Elephant in the Room

We spent time learning how to make each other laugh. Marc was fond of the art of punning. I would occasionally play the game. I was trying to learn the intersection between what he found funny and my sense of humor. *Killer Tomatoes* and the *Life of Brian* were not my taste. We could agree on *Monty Python and the Holy Grail* (although his enthusiasm was greater than mine) and we really came together on *The Hitchhiker's Guide to the Galaxy* and all things Douglas Adams.

"Oh, you have the complete audio files! That's awesome. Somewhere I have the complete BBC video production," I remembered but it was probably back in North Carolina.

"Oh, that's the best," Marc responded.

"As far as I'm concerned, he died too young."

"I totally agree."

"I once asked a librarian for recommendations for other authors like Douglas Adams. The librarian looked at me with sorrow in her eyes, shook her head and said,

"There are none."

"So true. I've never found anyone to compare," Marc agreed.

"They got the modern movie all wrong. Marvin the depressed robot should never be round and white!" I said with conviction.

"You are right - he wasn't in the BBC production."

"I always imagined him as black and rectilinear."

We laughed and traded opinions in great joy.

As "Big" said in *Sex and the City*, the one you stay with is the one that makes you laugh.

* * * * *

An elephant moved in upstairs with the other students who lived above us. He loved thumpy music with large subwoofer speakers on the floor, which made it untenable for me to meditate in the apartment whenever he was home, and he was home a lot. I tried headphones with meditation music to no avail. I requested he put towels under the speakers and, if he did it, it was no help at all.

Deciding that enough was already enough, we asked the Universe for another place to live. I think the Universe was a step ahead of us as we quickly found a wonderful little rental house on the north side of Phoenix for little more than the cost of the apartment. It was only 1,000 square feet but so well laid out that it felt much bigger. Three bedrooms and main part of the house had cathedral ceilings. The dining room had double glass doors that opened onto a patio with a barbeque which I used most of the time for cooking to keep the house cooler. The back yard was surrounded by block walls and I found no scorpions in the area, so it provided a safe run for Ms. Carley.

Before we had moved there a major fire took out most of the wooden walls between houses, which had been replaced by fireproof cinder block walls. Not attractive but much safer. Some homeowners planted bougainvillea to disguise them. It grew beautifully in this climate and it was one of the few things that did. I had always loved having house plants and had to leave many behind when I moved. The ones I kept were old friends, some I had for twenty years. The heat and dryness were more than they could bare and I completely understood.

The Glendale house was on the North side of Phoenix but our mailing address was Glendale. It was just inside the beltline and more convenient for escaping to Sedona which was usually ten to 15 degrees cooler. We made the move in July (JULY!) when it was 115°F and so dry you didn't even feel the sweat because It evaporated before it could run down your forehead. It was one of the most difficult moving experiences of my life but it was worth regaining peace and quiet.

I found places to walk Ms. Carley but none had the lovely water-filled canals of Dobson Ranch. One was a park with iguanas, one of which stood my car off with threatening gestures, puffing out its throat. I asked what its message was and understood it was alarmed at the increasing population surrounding the park. When you walked the South hill it was like something out of a science fiction novel. The landscape was rustic desert until you got to the hilltop where you saw the urban sprawl as far as the eye could see.

We made friends with the neighbors, especially the kids on our cul-de-sac who asked for support for their school fund raiser. Marc and I purchased things and by the time they brought them to us I had forgotten.

"Here's your cookie dough and ornaments," announced Sally.

"Oh, thank you so much."

I had just finished putting those things away and the doorbell rang again.

Sally and her friends stood at the door. Sally held a silly flamingo sculpture piece that looked like a refugee from a Florida Senior Center rummage sale.

"Nobody in this house would have bought that," I said feeling pretty sure of myself.

From over my shoulder, I heard a soft voice say,

"I would." I looked at Marc with surprise and said nothing. After thanking Anne and closing the door, I turned to Marc and said,

"Why would you buy that? It's so silly."

"Exactly," said Marc with a shy, apologetic smile.

I realized I had some judgments about silliness. What was it I felt? Too sophisticated, too mature, or maybe just too old? OK, I would work on letting go of that.

That night at dinner the Flamingo took center stage. I laughed. It was indeed silly.

"*Silly can be fun too,*" said my inner child. "*It can bring joy if you let it.*"

73

Chapter Seventeen
Crystal Clear

I continued to meditate during the day asking what I should be doing in the new quiet of our rental home. I was given various assignments to do healing work in many places. I was still trying to find work. I visited the metaphysical stores in the Phoenix Valley with no real openings. I started going up to Sedona to create relationships with store owners hoping for a place to do readings, Soul Integration and energy work. Marc and I drove up one Saturday and went into a new to me store. My attention was immediately drawn to a quartz crystal tower behind the cash register. It was calling to me. Eighteen inches tall, this tower looked like smokey quartz. It was beautiful but in distress. I curbed my impulse to jump over the counter to help the crystal and said,

"May I clear that crystal for you?"

"Yes, of course, please do," said the woman behind the counter.

I closed my eyes, focused on running love through the crystal and stayed in that mode for several minutes. When I felt complete, I opened my eyes. To my surprise the crystal was clear -- all the smokiness had disappeared. The clerk said, "Wait here please," and disappeared into a back room. She came out carrying a box of heavy green Chinese fluorite spheres.

"Whenever I put these out in the store, few customers come in. No one has ever picked one up and people avoid walking into the area where they are. I've moved them to various places in the store and it's always the same. That's why they've been in the far corner of the storeroom."

I closed my eyes and focused on the spheres which were physically attractive: medium bright greens with swirls of purple.

They did not feel attractive. As I focused asking in my heart what was up with these stones, a wide vision of a Chinese massacre formed in my imagination and I started sending peaceful loving energy into the stones. I asked for an energy of Five Flowers Remedy to be applied to remove the trauma. After some time in concentration, they felt clear.

"Thank you. I feel the difference. Please choose one of them for your service," said the woman who was now clearly the store owner or manager. I deferred to Marc to choose and he chose one of the smaller spheres.

We chatted with the owner and asked about places to do readings and healings. She told me she had readers and healers and didn't know anyone who needed someone at this time.

Later in the car I asked,

"Why did you pick the smallest sphere?"

"I don't know, it's the one that felt right."

"OK, I just wondered." Being a buyer and seller of crystals, I probably would have chosen one of the larger ones having the monetary value in mind. Marc chose based on what felt right, which is a better way to go. I appreciated his intuition. My respect was growing for this gentle man.

None of the other stores had any leads for work and I left disappointed. I should have felt joy at clearing the stones but I allowed the concern over what to do for work rob me of my joy.

Chapter Eighteen
Bi-Coastal

"Oh, hi, how are you? It's so nice to hear from you, Gwen." Gwen was a woman of few and direct words.

"It would be nice to see you, Lyneah. I need you to come back here and give me a massage. When are you coming back?"

"Well, I don't have any plans at this moment. There are plenty of massage therapists in Durham and Chapel Hill."

"I've tried a lot of them. No one is like you. I am tired of paying money to be disappointed. I need you. Please come back."

Several of these calls later, I objected by saying,

"Well, it's expensive to travel."

"Send out an email and ask how many would book a session with you. And pray on it. See if the Lord wants you to come back. I sure have been talking with Him about it myself."

"OK, I'll do that and let you know." Gwen was a person who did not take well to change.

I still had a small office in Durham which two other therapists were sub-leasing part time.

"I want first pick of my treatment time or times. I'll probably see you the first and last of the week you are here. Think about it, you could come back here for a week and see all of us and you could probably make money over and above your expenses."

"OK, I'll let you know Gwen. Thanks for calling and for your ideas."

The email resulted in a barrage of appointment requests. I scheduled the time so I could get Southwest's lowest fare and called Gwen.

"You were right, it's happening. Here are my dates, when do you want your appointments?"

"Goodie!" was her response. "There's no one like you. I can't wait."

Not everyone likes me but those who do are loyal customers.

This started my bicoastal lifestyle, which brought me great joy. I loved to fly and was quite grateful that enough people liked my work to make it worthwhile to go back. Not able to find work in Phoenix, I started going to North Carolina one week a month. It was a full schedule and hard work: I worked from ten in the morning until eight or nine at night, with breaks for lunch and dinner, six days in a row. There were new people referred by current clients I was not able to accommodate until the next month. My calendar filled for the next visit before I left. Being able to make a difference in other people's lives is a great source of joy. Gwen gladly booked her appointments for the next visit saying,

"I told you it would work. See you next month, my neck is so happy."

Chapter Nineteen
Lessons in Wisdom

Almost immediately after moving into the Glendale house, I flew to North Carolina to see my clients. I met a new client who was referred by another client.

"I asked the Lord to bring me a house for my birthday! It's my birthday today and I'm here to get a massage," Bess explained with a happy spirit.

"I have a house for sale." I confessed.

"What's it like?" she asked.

"It's a log cabin and has a quarter acre with it. It has new HVAC, new electrical, I've restored all the logs and stained it a beautiful brown…" I continued to explain all the renovations and Bess listened intently.

"Could we go see it after the massage?"

"Well, yes, we could." I responded since my lunch break followed.

I was staying with Maria, so I had not been to the cabin yet this trip. It had been several months but Jim was staying there in exchange for care taking the place. When we walked in, I was shocked. The ceiling was hanging down in three rooms. The kitchen was totally unusable. The man who was supposed to be taking care of my place was instead letting it go. Every time I called him, he had said everything was fine. We had a heated interaction over the phone and a slightly more heated exchange when he showed up. I stood up to him knowing something was not right. He gruffly took his stuff, threw down a key and I called immediately to have the locks changed.

I heard Jim resentfully say to a neighbor as he left,
"She's gone and sold it to somebody else."
I couldn't hear the neighbor's reply but got the clear download that they were in cahoots. They planned to let the house get so I would sell it to them cheap. Then they planned on combining the properties to build a small apartment complex like the one on the other side. They would make a bunch of money leaving me out of the deal and probably making me feel they had done me a favor by taking the 'dump' off my hands. Furry flamed through me. I had completed major renovations, much of them by my own hand here before I left, other changes I contracted. The house had been in pristine condition when I left. There was nothing I could do but it seemed things would work out despite their worst efforts.

Bess was sympathetic and, to my surprise, still interested in the house as it met her criteria perfectly. My insurance would cover the repairs. She would rent the house until she could get a mortgage. We had papers drawn up.

In the attic I found the source of the water. The contractor who installed the HVAC was someone I felt sorry for. This was an expensive lesson that led to a sign in my office which reminds me:

"When you enable someone to be dysfunctional, you pay."

He had been difficult and inconsistent in installing, not showing up on time and not answering my calls. It took twice the time it should have. He finally offered a long sob story and said he would give me a lifetime guarantee on his work, so I let him finish the job, cancelling the other contractor I had called. This man installed the drip pan drain for the system incorrectly and the result was a leak large enough to destroy part of the ceiling in three rooms. It turns out he was a heroin addict and had the name of a major HVAC family in the area but was the black sheep thrown out of the. I didn't learn this until I found out he had overdosed leaving me with a worthless lifetime guarantee.

The woman, Bess, had a brother who was a contractor and he agreed to do the work. I had already called a friend whose husband was a handyman and they came to correct the immediate problem in the drain.

My last day at the office I had an incident with plumbers in an office down the hall making racial slurs and sexual innuendos while I had a black male client on the table. Their children repeatedly ran to the door and made loud noises. The parents did nothing in response to my request for quiet. I was shocked and complained to the manager who was completely unhelpful. I decided to move out and they quickly agreed to give me a refund for the part of the month I would not be using. Someone else wanted the space and the Universe was telling me I was done here, so I sold what I didn't need and packed what I did. There were other offices who would share space with me when I returned and this would save me the monthly rent. This way in the future I would only pay for the time I used.

With all that taken care of in three weeks' time, I packed house and office into a U-Haul and made the trek across the country again but on a slightly different route. This time I went through Midland-Odessa. Now I know it's the Gary, Indiana of Texas and not a route I would willingly repeat. I also knew why Valorie didn't live there anymore. The air quality was dreadful. My eyes teared even with AC and recycled air.

Faywood Mineral Springs was again a great stop after 2,000 miles. I enjoyed the hot springs and rejuvenated in the energy of the place. I did not, however, have the springs to myself this time which emphasized how special the last visit had been. I was drawn to a beautiful layered green stone and placed it in the passenger seat of the U-Haul. I left full of gratitude and joy.

Reuniting with Marc was a huge source of joy. It was so nice to be together again. Distance did make the heart grow fonder.

Chapter Twenty
No Happy Ending

Once back in Arizona, I investigated doing outcalls now that I had my massage table and supplies. I went to many different hotels leaving my cards. At one of the bigger hotels, I was told to give it to the Head Porter in the entranceway. He looked at my card and asked,

"What kind of massage do you do?"

I answered,

"Strictly therapeutic massage…" and I don't think he heard a word after that.

He put the card absentmindedly in his pocket and said we'll call if we need you. Later I learned that he looked for people who gave 'Happy Ending' massages and it turned out that Phoenix was famous for providing these services to the many golfers and businessmen the area drew. Happy Ending massages got much larger tips and the Head Porter got half.

I got a call from a man in town with six buddies for golf. He said they needed seven massages. I told him it was therapeutic massage and he said OK. When I completed his massage, he asked if I was done.

"Yes, unless there's something else you need," I added.

He pointed at his groin and I shook my head no. Not only did he want me to give him a happy ending but he wanted me to do it in front of the other guys in the suite. I'm sure he expected me to do it for all seven of them! I was shocked. I went to the bathroom and washed my hands trying to wash off the icky energy. When I came back, he was dressed. He paid me for the massage adding a small tip. I packed up and left. He said he'd call for the others. I probably don't even need to tell you the phone never rang.

I had one hotel call me for a woman and her daughter who came every three weeks for a special therapy. They became my only regular massage clients. Two massages every three weeks would not support me.

"I am so frustrated. I am not finding work. Even Manpower has not found anything for me."

"Don't be discouraged. Your meditations have been important and we have started on the Embracing Worthiness CD and that should open some doors."

"I don't have the resources to open my own massage office and I won't work for the low wages other places offer and out calls are not happening."

"Why not look into teaching metaphysical classes? Your Soul Integration work, energy healing, past life healing could be done at a metaphysical shop. You could also do card readings with the Crystal Ally cards."

I continued visiting many metaphysical stores in the Valley and in Sedona and most were not interested for one or another reason.

Finally, at the Rainbow Connection, a metaphysical store in the Phoenix Valley, I found some interest. We arranged for me to teach a crystal class. Attendance was excellent, filling the long tables in a back room. I started with the ways to clear crystals.

"Set your intention…" a hand at the back of the room interrupted me. "Yes," I said indicating the lady with the raised hand.

"What's intention?"

I thought for a moment and gave an answer about will forces and what you want and talked about using these forces to clear the crystals. Some blank faces indicated some had no idea what I was talking about. How could I teach a group who was largely not in touch with their intentions?

I completed the discussion and moved to other methods of clearing crystals such as bringing them into the shower with you and putting them out in the full moon or out in the sunshine.

"Should you put them in saltwater?" one participant asked.

"My guidance has generally been not to use that method for crystals it is too strong for them. I use Epsom salts to clear my basalt hot stones for massage and they seem happy with it but my crystals have told me they don't like it."

I was given guidance on the spot that I could make an elixir that could be used to clear crystals and when I mentioned it to the group, they were enthusiastic. I promised to bring some to the store to be sold there.

The elixir sold well but they were never interested in me doing another presentation. One of the friends I made out of that presentation was a healer named Gisela and when I talked with her and mentioned that the connection there just fizzled she said,

"Of course, they are all air signs and you are a pretty strong earth with little or no air in your chart. It is harder to connect and communicate because of this. The owner is almost pure air and she draws air signs to her. There was nothing wrong with your presentation, it was good."

"Thank you for that. I was concerned I had done something wrong."

"No, they actually liked your presentation, it's just that it is not a natural fit. It is not personal. "

"But you are an air sign, why do we get along?"

"Oh yes, I am air but I have some earth in my chart which makes it easier. Air signs are drawn to the desert because we love the open air and we don't need a lot of earth or water in our lives. You are different you need both earth and the kind of earth that grows green things and you need a lot of water. I have wondered why you were here in the desert."

"Me too."

Gisela was the first person I really felt connected with and we became good friends and exchanged healings at her house and mine. I attended group healing exchanges at her house and after a time, I asked if she would write a testimonial for me and this is what she wrote:

"Each session was a great teaching session for me as a healer. Lyneah lifts me to a higher dimension. I am seeing visions more clearly. Lyneah opened the Akashic records for me and now I can see them on my own. I have learned techniques which profoundly

change the energy of my past lives. Each session I have opened up to more clarity, more empowerment, and a deeper spiritual awareness. You have brought out in me the potentials that are really there -- ones that I didn't even know about. I never knew you could go this far with the work. I am at a higher level. Lyneah is an awesome healer and a great teacher. Fully open to the possibilities of me being my best and all that is for the highest good."

Gisela Arenas, Quantum Angel Healing Practitioner, Tempe, AZ
*

I know I wrote as glowing a testimonial for Gisela but I don't have a copy of that now.

Another person I met at this presentation was Heather Clarke who started the Arizona Enlightenment Center. She invited me to Goodyear to give the same crystal class to the Enlightenment Center which did not yet have a permanent home. It met at various places including Heather's living room. This class was a delight to teach and I met many people who became friends. One started helping me with my website CoraLynn Hughes. This finally seemed to be a good fit. There was great joy in finally finding a place in the Valley and having friends makes all the difference. It doesn't take many, but having real friends fills my heart to overflowing with joy.

Chapter Twenty-One
Flamingo Paste

Preparing for Thanksgiving, I made what had become my traditional cranberry sauce. It's a thick pink preparation made from sour cream (or yogurt), onions, horseradish, sugar (honey) and of course organic fresh cranberries. Originally, I made this sauce to prove Susan Stanberg on NPR wrong. Every year before Thanksgiving she announced her grandmother's cranberry recipe and how good it was. I was more than skeptical. One year I made it to prove her wrong but she was right, it is not only delicious, it is addictive. I have made it every year since. Later Susan announced the recipe dated back to an issue of the LA Times.

One of Marc's colleagues joined us for Thanksgiving dinner this year. He and Marc talked about one of the contracts that they had worked on and they had a running joke that if they couldn't figure out what was wrong with the machine it needed Flamingo paste. Shortly after one of their stories, I brought the cranberry sauce to the table.

"It's the mysterious Flamingo paste!" announced Alan.

The Flamingo statue was, of course, on the table as well partially because I could not find fall-colored leaves. I had searched the Phoenix valley in vain for colored leaves and one weekend, we drove north of Sedona to the overlook atop the Mogollon Rim where the view is huge. The entire vista had only one maple tree in color and it was not accessible. Otherwise, the only color was the yellow of the golden aspens. A few weeks earlier, I had seen colored leaves for sale at a craft store. I scoffed at them thinking I could find my own. Now that I was clearly wrong about that, I returned the next day and they were sold out.

We had many laughs over dinner. Alan was as geekish as Marc and they had many in jokes involving shows and experiences unfamiliar to me. I discovered, somewhat to my dismay, they could both quote the *Holy Grail*, *The Princess Bride* and *Pinky and the Brain* verbatim almost in their entireties. When Alan separated from his wife, he moved into our place for a time.

I learned that timing was everything in getting Marc to really laugh hard. I needed to wait for times when something absurd could be said at just the right moment, usually a beat or two after it might be expected. You really need to be there to appreciate the full effect but one example happened before Mother's Day. Only a geek would decide you needed a new Mother Board for your Mother's Day present! I was grateful for his diagnostic skills. I had not yet learned the obsolescence factor in computers and I had kept this one alive with the help of a few computer techs along the way.

"You've already kept this thing going for way longer than most people would," Marc informed me with a raised wild eyebrow.

"But I'm used to it and I love it and I don't want a new computer."

"OK then, let me buy you a new Mother Board for Mother's Day."

"Really? You'll be able to make her go again?"

"Yes. How long do you keep your cars?"

I realized I did tend to hold on to things. Each one of my cars had a name and I generally got more mileage than expected out of each one.

"OK, I see your point. But I think there is something else we could do."

"Oh, what is that?" asked Marc skeptically.

"I'll be right back." I walked into the kitchen, opened the fridge and searched for the yogurt container that held the leavings from the last batch of Cranberry sauce. I took it into the living room, opened it, tipped the opening toward Marc and exclaimed,

"Flamingo paste!!!!!"

Chapter Twenty-Two
Hyundai

One morning, I was awakened in a less gentle fashion than usual. There was a sense of urgency that made me go straight for the meditation chair and skip nature's calling for the time being. I asked,

"*What do you need*?"

"*PRAY!!! PRAY HARD!!!!!!!!!!!!!!!!!!!!!!!!!!!*" came the urgent response. Before I could formulate the word 'how', an image of using great strength-of-will to form a cloud of energy that could be used for whatever was going on formed in my mind. I followed instructions and created this cloud of energy, feeling non-physical guides and angels taking the energy somewhere.

In another room far away from my meditation, my phone rang. By the time I got to it the call had hung up. It was Alexandrea's number. I called back immediately. She was three hours ahead and would have been going to work at this time. A crying upset voice answered the phone in Roswell, Georgia.

"MOM!!! My car is wrecked and the Goo Goo Dolls CD they signed for me is stuck in the CD player. I Can't get it out. Where were you?" I saw in my mind's eye a gnarly accident scene.

"How are you?" Are you hurt?"

"Oh, no, I don't think so. I'm OK but my car and my CD…"

"Please go to the hospital and get checked out."

"Oh, I don't think that's necessary, I'm fine."

"Adrenalin has kicked in and you can't tell if you are hurt at this point. The car is replaceable; you have insurance and the CD, well you can get another and maybe get them to sign it somehow. You are not replaceable." I started running peaceful healing energy for her and listened while she described how the large Toyota Tundra truck came crashing through the intersection, smashing into the front passenger side of her Hyundai while she was waiting to execute a left turn. She talked fast until the police arrived and she had to go.

After the call I wondered,

"*What would have happened if I had not answered this morning's call to meditation?*" There was no immediate answer but an uneasy feeling in my stomach and a large set of chills. It provided me with greater motivation to listen even more attentively and follow instructions without hesitation especially when being awakened at any hour.

Chapter Twenty-Three
Making the Wheel

Getting up from my meditation, I called Marc and said,

"We're supposed to go to Verde Valley to find the creator stone for a Medicine Wheel. Now that we have a back yard, we have space for a wheel."

"Interesting. That's a little like being told to go to find a quarter in Rhode Island." After a smiling pause, he continued,

"We could start this weekend."

"OK, I'll check some things out online and see if I can narrow it down a bit."

When Marc got home from work, we discussed the assignment.

"There is a hot spring on the river up there and that's what I'm drawn to."

"Of course you are, my love." Marc looked at the map and said,

"OK, we'll take the dog with us, she'll enjoy the walk."

On the way to Verde Valley, we stopped at a gas station that had a rustic metal statue of a bull more than two stories tall. Carley headed right for its heels and tried to nip it to herd it into place!!!!!! Her herding instinct knew no bounds. It took considerable coaxing to get her away from the statue.

We headed for the river, had a nice long walk up the river but never found the springs. Driving out the road I heard:

"*Stop!*"

Before I could say it out loud, Marc hit the brakes. We smiled and I asked,

"You heard it too, didn't you?"

Marc nodded, backed up and said, "It's about here."

I got out of the car and walked directly to a large rock with a dark streak forming a cross on the top. I asked if it was the creator stone and got a big '*yes*'. I lifted it, put it in the back of the Subaru and Marc said,

"It feels right."

"So, with the help of Spirit, we can find a needle in a haystack." I observed. Marc smiled his agreement. It felt so good to have a partner who was willing to listen to his intuition and I was grateful to have the confirmation.

In the next weeks I was guided to many different areas to collect stones for the medicine wheel. Some came from high energy parts of Sedona, others from Pleasant Lake and Tonopah. One was collected at Faywood Mineral Springs. Twenty-eight stones in all. We were using the book *Dancing with the Wheel* by Marlise Wabun Wind, Sun Bear and Crysalis Mulligan. A group came out from North Carolina for a class and we placed the stones into the form for the wheel. It went surprisingly quickly, which was part of the non-traditional aspect of this wheel. It was a blend of old and new. So were the ceremonies. Guided, they had some traditional aspects and some more modern elements. It felt right for our time and we started doing ceremonies in the wheel. I could feel the energy building in it and it grew steadily over time. The back yard felt new and joy came to my smile as I tuned into the growing energy.

Chapter Twenty-Four
In Search of Enlightenment

"Here, this is for you," spoke one of my clients, standing with her husband next to a display cabinet poking out of the back of their truck bed. "My husband found it by the side of the road and was told to pick it up and bring it to you."

"That's interesting; I don't know where I'm going to put it. and I don't know why I need it but I asked and got,

"*Yes, take it.*"

That happened in Durham, before I even had a thought of moving to Arizona. When we loaded the truck in North Carolina, strong guidance indicated I was to bring the display case with me. I stored it in the garage, still not knowing what to do with it. It was glass on the top and sides, with two glass half shelves and a full floor with wooden storage space underneath. I had no plans to open a store here despite the urgings of one of Marc's friends.

The Arizona Enlightenment Center had become a source of inspiration: a place to meet people, a place to offer energy healing work, Soul Integration including past life healings, teaching classes and leading ceremonies. The center had moved into a renovated gas station building. It had many rooms which we converted into treatment rooms, a large room for group meetings and space for a store near the front. Many people helped. It was a community of healers and those interested in healing paint and ready the place. Two members started the store. I walked in to see if I could help and said,

"Oh, I know exactly what goes in that space." The cabinet from North Carolina fit perfectly and was just what they were looking for. They placed the expensive items in this case since it locked.

Jewelry on the upper glass half shelf, small hand-made items and small crystals on the next and larger heavier items on the wooden bottom. It looked stunning when complete. I smiled thinking how this cabinet made its way here and mused on the workings of spirit.

The center had a code lock on the front door and many people had the code. Inside, the gift shop had a separate lock and only the three shopkeepers had a key. Open wooden shelves to the right of the door had rows of homeopathic bottles ten across and five deep. Opening the shop one morning, Terry found a neat row of bottles on the floor in front of the wooden shelves. One of each of ten bottles stood on the floor in a neat row. Checking the shelf, she found each row had four bottles exactly where they belonged. The bottles on the floor had to be the last bottles from each row behind the undisturbed bottles.

"*Curious*," she thought. While returning the bottles to the shelf, she pondered why anyone would do that. She didn't have a hypothesis and kept the incident to herself.

The next day another of the shopkeepers, Joy, opened the store and found a glass tabletop overturned with all the hand-painted scarves and small pocketbooks upside down in the middle of the floor. She called Terry, who had locked up the night before and received assurance everything was in order at the time she left. She explained about finding the bottles on the floor the morning before.

Terry made sure all things were in order when she left that night; she came in and opened the next morning, to find all the items from the second shelf inside the locked cabinet overturned onto the shelf below. Nothing was broken. This time a little freaked out, she called the director, who told her to call me.

"What do you want me to do?" I asked.

"Heather said you would know what to do," said Terry, a little nervously.

"OK I'll see what I can do."

In meditation I asked who was there and did not have to wait long. A thirty-something good-looking dark-haired man presented himself in my inner sight.

"*What do you want?*" I asked calmly.

"*I want Enlightenment, of course, you are the Enlightenment Center, aren't you?*" he asked with an edge of annoyance. "*I've been trying to get your attention for a while now.*"

This brought a smile.

"*How can we provide enlightenment for you?*"

He communicated through images now -- automobile accident on the nearby highway indicating he died in the crash. His distress over how his family was doing without him was his major concern. He didn't know how to find them. I tuned in, asked my guides to help me and found the Akashic Records of his family since his death. I showed them to him and when he saw his family had gone through their mourning and were doing fine now, he relaxed and realized it was ok. I felt a rush of emotions followed by relief. Calm followed.

"*Are you willing to cross over now?*" I asked.

He nodded his consent. I asked angels to help him and spiritual beings opened a portal of golden yellow light and helped him across. It felt very peaceful and the Enlightenment Center had no further poltergeist activity. There was a great sense of joy at being able to help a spirit in distress find peace. What an amazing thing to be able to do for someone. I was then guided to clear the area of the accident along the highway and saw in inner sight a dark cloud turn bright. I sat in a prayer of gratitude feeling great joy.

* * * * *

When I give talks about ghosts, it amazes me how many people come up to me after with their own stories. Society, science and logic says there are no such things as ghosts but experience tells us otherwise. In *Thirsting for a Raindrop,* I described the first time I saw a ghost. I was little, too little to go down the stairs alone. I remember holding my mother's hand and the railing and being very deliberate and careful descending the stairs to my Aunt Harriet's basement. I thought my mother had gotten "fat" – she was not fat -- she was pregnant with my younger brother born when I was 18 months old. So, I was less than 18 months at the time and narrowing it down further, it was Thanksgiving. I was born mid-September, so I was one year and three months old when I remember seeing my first ghost. I think seeing ghosts is a little like color. Some people see all sorts of colors, others are color blind. Some people see ghosts and others are ghost blind.

In graduate school at West Virginia University (WVU), I taught in the Physical Science Department.

"I don't believe in ghosts," a white lab-coated PhD candidate, who had far more training in physics than I did, remarked one day.

"Why?" I inquired.

"Because I don't know anything that will go through a brick wall and rattle chains on the other side," he pointed at the wall for emphasis. Mulling on this a bit, I responded,

"Well, correct me if I'm wrong, if I had an electromagnetic field generator and I projected a field through the wall and oscillated it, would it not rattle chains on the other side?" He turned quite pale and didn't speak to me for weeks.

Our sciences can measure things like ghosts and energy bodies, we just don't have the construct, as Piaget would call it. It is only 200 years since people were jailed and killed for outrageous ideas such as the sun is the center of the Galaxy and only recently have church and science separated. Science is not willing to get back in bed with religion, so it has steadfastly avoided anything that might indicate the existence of a soul because that might invite religion back in the door and heresy, hence punishment, might return. Breakthrough scientists have been attempting to dismantle these walls in the past few decades.

We are generally frightened of ghosts. Why? Well, movies and stories have sensationalized the idea and the ones that are scary have made the greatest impression. What comes to mind when I say the word ghost? Something terrible that can hurt you? Aunt Bessie? *Casper the Friendly Ghost*? *Ghostbusters*? Most of the images are frightening. Funny as it was, *Ghostbusters* showed some scary spirits.

There are friendly ghosts who are often relatives who have died.

They often have messages. Mine come most frequently at holidays or special events such as weddings, deaths, illness and births. This past Easter I felt a chill and a friend who was with me felt it too. She asked who that was and I turned inward to find a line of my relatives coming to say hello and to provide comfort. It was sweet. At my brother's wedding there was an apparently empty space to the right of center at the front. Several people suggested family fill in that space but most knew it was already occupied. My cousin and niece both commented that our deceased relatives were standing in that space. It's interesting that everyone, whether they were able to see ghosts or not, left that space open for the entire ceremony.

There are lost ghosts – some call them disembodied spirits. They are people who have died but often they died suddenly and they are generally looking for something. This was the type of ghost in the movie *The Sixth Sense* and the Enlightenment center's poltergeist.

By request, I started teaching classes on how to clear ghosts and I often get requests to clear ghosts from houses and businesses. Many realtors have hired me to clear properties that would not sell. I call it ECE: Energy Clearing and Elevation. It's not just about clearing, it's also about raising the vibration level to one that benefits the third dimensional occupants. Some businesses have hired me to clear them once a month and after major events. It is beneficial to clear a house after illness. My house really needed clearing after my divorce.

"Do you watch the ghost hunters on TV?" asked one of my students.

"No, I don't watch most of them because they are sensational and looking to stimulate fear. They have no consideration for lost souls and no thought of how to help them. This is also largely true of the scientific groups who hunt ghosts to use their equipment trying to prove their existence. They too have little thought of how to help these lost souls. It brings me great joy to help them."

Chapter Twenty-Five
Ceremonies

I was asked to do a Burning Bowl Ceremony at the Arizona Enlightenment Center after the new year. I agreed and did some research. Fire in the desert is, of course, a significant concern especially in the dry season. We chose a metal barbeque to contain the fire despite the fact that I knew Native Americans do not believe that you should build fires in metal but this was not a purely native ceremony but a combination. I also do not like the burning of sage or any kind of smoke, especially in an enclosed space; I prefer using a sage spray. Most often I use my rattle to clear space. This is a beautiful handmade rattle filled with high vibration crystals.

A Native American man came to this ceremony and I was nervous at his presence, fearful of not living up to his expectations. I had talked with him a couple of times at the center and attended one of his classes on Kabala. He was very nice but I feared his judgment because my ceremony was not traditional. I took many deep breaths and preceded with the ceremony in the way I had been guided. The first thing was to clear participants one at a time using the crystal rattle. When I finished clearing the Native man, he looked at me and said,

"That really works!" which helped me relax a little more.

After the entire process and the closing ceremony at the fire I went up to him to ask what he thought about the it.

"Fire is fire, metal is metal and water is water," he said somewhat automatically, then looked at me in surprise. He explained that this was his guidance coming through and that traditionally fire was not put in metal. He said that the ancestors approved of the way I did the ceremony despite its blend of traditional and modern methods. I was surprised, relieved and grateful for his feedback.

I felt encouraged to continue doing ceremonies and New Moon Ceremonies were one of my favorites.

The dark of the moon is when you perform New Moon Ceremony. It is to help you manifest what you want in your life. After listening to the qualities that are most favorable for that month, you write your requests and place them energetically into the dark of the moon in ceremony there to be gestated as the moon waxes. It is a good time to focus on what you want in life and when you do it monthly it helps you pay attention to what has come into your life. If you are interested in this, consult the book, *New Moon Astrology* by Jan Spiller. I found I had to change her wording to be more positive and eliminate the "want to" phrasings. It is more powerful to speak what you want as if you already have it – saying 'I have all the resources I need' rather than 'I want all the resources I need'. My personal interest in the New Moon Ceremonies I led in North Carolina had been to find a life partner. It seems they worked.

Chapter Twenty-Six
The King's Castle

After settling my furniture into the new house, it felt more like home. Now having space and furniture I was ready to have a gathering. I invited some of my new friends over for a meditation. Marc had been downloading music, I downloaded the meditations in real time and this gathering would give us a chance to practice working together with a live audience.

Serving refreshments afterward, Marc hovered nervously about. When the last person left, he walked toward me full of issues. I could read it clearly. This was his castle and it had been invaded. I could see this was going to be a deal breaker for me. Marc barely began lodging his complaint when I responded,

"This is who I am. I am gregarious. I have people over to my home. If you can't deal with that, you can't be with me. Let me know if I need to find another place to live." I returned to the kitchen to clean up.

Marc stewed a bit but realized this was indeed a critical issue for me. I knew what it felt like to be with someone who wanted to annihilate the essence of who I am, replace it with some ideal woman and I was not going to stand for that again. We sat down and had an adult, even-tempered conversation and we both showed understanding. Marc conveyed his concerns, discomfort and his willingness to try to come out of his introverted shell if I could be patient. I agreed to work on it from my side to be considerate and let him know ahead of time. I wondered how someone who wanted to be a performer could be such an introvert. I was no longer willing to lose myself in a relationship but I was willing to be considerate and to compromise. There was joy in working this through knowing we both had enough interest in making this work. I was still willing to split if we needed to but there was more joy in knowing we still had a chance and that we were developing the tools to work things through.

Chapter Twenty-Seven
Have Sagittarius will Travel

"Hello, handsome." I greeted Marc without looking up from dinner preparations, until he didn't respond and I sensed the grey cloud his mood had ushered in.

"What's up?" I asked and turned fully toward him in concern.

"My contract has been terminated at the grain company. They are shifting their focus and 'no longer need my services'."

"Well, in a way that's good news because it means you don't have to work for that mean guy anymore. Mr. Marine will no longer be in your life. Hurray."

I tried to put a positive spin on this event, feeling that it was for the best for all of us. I didn't know what was coming but I had faith that it would be good. I have noticed in my life that it is a waste of time to feel bad after you have been liberated from a job - voluntarily or otherwise - and that you should take advantage of the time because your in-between time might be short and you should enjoy it to the fullest while you can.

We talked over dinner and decided that since we had adequate savings, we would go on a trip that we had been guided to take. Marc was the orienteer and often got spiritual guidance on where we were supposed to go.

Mt. Shasta, Oregon and the California coast were the first destinations. I was excited about Mt. Shasta and the Redwoods and seeing our friend Tom in Oregon. This was to be both an Earth healing trip and a personal healing trip. The various elevations would yield from 100+ degrees to snow, so we'd had to pack for dressing in layers.

"I might find something in the way of work on this trip," Marc offered.

I looked at him. He had only been in Phoenix one year and now he was ready to move again. I was not. I thought this over and later started the conversation.

"How many places have you lived?"

Marc offered a long list of places.

"What's the longest you have stayed in one place?"

"In my adult life?"

"Yes, childhood doesn't count here."

After some mental review, he responded,

"Two years."

"Two years! Wow, that doesn't work for me. It takes me two years to establish a client base to support me. If you have a need to move every two years, I don't think this is going to work for us."

So far, we had worked through the stoppers. Later that evening, Marc said he was willing to try to stay in one place longer.

"I think you would agree Arizona is not that place," he concluded.

"Agreed," I said with some relief.

It was late November 2004. We were off to Mt. Shasta first. The trip there was lovely, snow having been cleared off the roads. Mount Shasta is a 14,000+ foot mountain that can be seen from 100 miles away on a clear day. It is snow-crested most of the year but the amount has been decreasing with global warming. Excitement raised in my belly as we neared the mountain, its energy affecting us from a distance. This was the first time I'd returned to Mt. Shasta since the portal opening in 2003. There had already been several snows this year.

We found our hotel, settled in, donned our silk long underwear, winter boots, hats, gloves and scarves and headed up to Bunny Flats at just shy of 7,000 feet. The parking lot was full and many happy voices rang out: sledding children whooping in joy, skiers, snow boarders, snowshoers and some with only boots to keep them going. We trekked up the snow-covered road above Bunny Flats avoiding the skiers coming down. The parking lot ended at a wall of snow at least six feet high. The sun was bright and the mountain amazing in its white skirt. Quite the difference from Phoenix!

Back in town we picked up hot drinks at Yak's and started to walk around the corner to a shop called Mount Shasta's Middle Earth Crystal Room. (Now The Crystal Room, Crystal Tones at Mount Shasta.) It was a store a friend had highly recommended as the best in town. Outside the store, the owner, holding strings of Christmas lights was talking with two young men who seemed to be helping her. When I tried to move around them to go into the store, she blocked my way and caught my eye.

"May I come in?" I asked.

"We are closed today. I'm only here to do Christmas decorations; come back tomorrow."

"I'm sorry, we won't be here tomorrow. We must leave first thing in the morning."

She looked us over, closed her eyes and in a short time said:

"Please come in. I'll be with you in a moment."

I was sure she had asked if it was right action. Beverly, as I later learned her name, handed the lights over, gave directions to the helpers and brought us into the store. What followed was an amazing gift. We learned we had a lot in common. Beverly had also been involved with Rudolf Steiner's work and I told her that I had been a Waldorf Teacher. She led us through room after room pointing out particular crystals and asking us to hold some of them. She continued to a room where she asked us to watch while she turned a large rutilated quartz on a stand. She turned it nine times.

"That's the most it's ever asked me to rotate it for anyone," said Beverly with raised eyebrows. I didn't know what that meant exactly, but I felt honored and inwardly thanked the crystal.

What followed was an extensive healing concert using a wide variety of crystal bowls including some with gold and others with moldavite. We sat on a rug in the center of the room wondering why we were so privileged. She brought out crystal tuning forks and used them on us as we laid on the floor. The last one was surprisingly large, more than four feet long! Its vibrations went up and down my spine and tingled my entire body. Next, in a backroom we were treated to the joy of a large collection of high energy andaran crystals some of which we purchased. Andaran

105

crystals are like obsidian but formed by interdimensional activity rather than volcanic. Both are natural forms of glass highly energized. Like obsidian they come in many colors. Ours were brown and green.

We showed her the CD's we brought with us. Marc's music CDs and the meditation CD set to his music: *Embracing Worthiness*. She took some of each on consignment after listening to them on her stereo system.

As we paid for the Andarans, we asked if we owed her anything for all her time and treatments. She shook her head no.

"Thank you for a most extraordinary day. We feel so grateful for all you did." I disclosed with a heart overflowing with joy and gratitude.

"My pleasure. It was meant to be."

"That may be," I thought, *"but why?"*

Thanking Beverly again we went to find food to ease our growling stomachs.

Up on the mountain one more time that night we admired the stars and did a meditation. We wondered if St. Germain would appear this time but there was just a soft, gentle indication of his presence. Nothing dramatic. We slept especially well that night.

In the morning we left early and the drive to Ashland was scary, proceeding very slowly through freezing fog. Going over the Siskiyou Summit at 4,300 feet with steep downhill curves and heavy truck traffic is a feat under normal circumstances. Interstate 5 is the only way across into Oregon. There are no other routes, the other mountains are not passable except through this summit. Normally a broad vista, we could not see down into the valley at all. Slowly crawling along listening to the freezing droplets hitting the windshield our visibility was a few feet at best. We made it to Ashland in one piece and rested over breakfast.

Continuing the drive, we went through Grants Pass to the Oregon National Caves Monument where my friend Tom on time. I met Tom in North Carolina and he now worked for the Park Service here. The caves were closed, so we walked the forest enjoying the outdoors. Tom's dog trotted by our side, ran off and came back whenever Tom called. We drove on to Crescent City, stopping to hug the giant Redwoods along the way. It was already dark and the giants looked magnificent in the shadows of the night! Awestruck is what I felt connecting with their powerful energies. I do love trees and have some that are friends in every place I've lived. These giants would have to become friends too. We would have liked to stay longer, but something was pressing us onward.

We overnighted in Crescent City. The next morning, we visited many Redwoods along the coast. What majestic trees they are!

Arcata was our next stop, a quaint town square being the center of commerce. Each store had its own charm. The weather was mild and sunny. We met some friends Marc had met at the West Coast Mystery School. Their bookstore was right on the square.

"Arcata has passed an ordinance to keep big box stores out. This makes it easier on the local store owners. So many big box stores have run the smaller businesses out of other towns," explained the bookstore owners.

"What about the Redwoods?" I asked. There were none in the town though the area before the town was a full redwood forest.

"It used to be all Redwoods but they have been cut. I don't mind so much because it changed the environment from a rain forest to sunny days. The Redwoods create their own climate drawing much rain and they make it very dark."

It may have also contributed to the lack of rain," I thought but not being certain about that I didn't say anything. I felt so sad at the devastation of so many of the Redwoods. How thoughtless to cut giant trees that took Mother Nature hundreds of years to grow.

We left after lunch and headed South. In Sebastopol we found a metaphysical store interested in carrying our CDs.

Marc was particularly fond of San Francisco shown by his smile and his light mood. He had memories of good times in previous lives there. Interesting to me because he was phobic about other parts of the coast. We spent time at Fisherman's Warf amid the throngs of seagulls ready to take whatever scraps we might leave behind. We watched the seals at the ocean front, ate in Chinatown and drove some of the more famous streets. I was so grateful to have been able to see so much beauty on this trip, both natural and manmade. I had already seen the museums here and that was not something Marc was interested in, so we stayed outside.

It seemed like a normal trip until we began to drive down the Peninsula along California 35, Skyline Drive. It was a beautiful drive and the grass was green this time of year; it reminded me of what I thought Ireland must look like.

Suddenly my stomach became tight and I felt strong waves of anxiety for no apparent reason. Marc was concerned but did not have the same sensations. I went into meditation and asked what was up,

"There is an earthquake brewing right beneath you. You are traveling over the San Andreas Fault." The answer came clearly.

"Why did you send us here?"

"If you do your work, it will not happen."

Highly motivated I asked,

"What do we need to do?" an image of a large crescent-shaped sore at the southern end of the San Francisco Bay appeared in my imagination. The impression was that much negative energy had gathered in this area and created this wound.

"Cauterize the wound," was the instruction I received.

I immediately called Maria at work on her cell phone. She was a busy physician and never answered her phone at work.

"Hello, this is Maria," her voice rang out.

"I need help. We are to cauterize a wound in the south end of San Francisco Bay to stop an earthquake from happening. We are driving directly over it. I thought immediately of you because you are a physician. Please help - if we don't do it correctly there will be an earthquake and we may be right in the middle of it."

We went to work as Marc steadily drove and held space and she saw the wound in her internal vision. She described it just as I had seen it. After we cauterized it, my stomach returned to neutral and the anxiety disappeared just as suddenly as it had started. We asked just to make sure,

"Is this complete? Is there anything else that we need to do?"

"Well done," is what we all heard.

Afterwards, I had greater empathy for hamsters running madly around their wheels before earthquakes. Checking the map later we found we were driving directly over the San Andreas Fault!

During the entire ten-day trip there was nothing that called to us for work or a place to live. The clearing of the earthquake seemed to be one of the main reasons for this trip, aside from all the beauty and energy we experienced and the healing at the Crystal Shop in Mt. Shasta. We returned to Phoenix across hours and hours of desert. If I ever see another Joshua tree again, it'll be too soon.

We wondered what we were going to do for work. Now, if we could only find a way to be paid for the earth healing work. This was the third time we'd been told we had stopped an earthquake in the San Francisco area. If we could get paid for this, we wouldn't need other work.

Reflecting on this trip, I wonder if Beverly prepared us to do this work when we visited her crystal shop in Mt. Shasta. The thought brought a wave of gratitude through my heart space. Even when we don't know it, we work together. When we are listening and dedicated to the highest good of all. Great, great flood of joy!

Chapter Twenty-Eight
Monkey Business

I was introduced to a chiropractor who was referred to me as someone interested in alternatives. Since I worked part time in a chiropractor's office in North Carolina, I thought this might be an option for work. He asked me one day, when I was waiting to see him, to do something with his client and her daughter. He said he was unable to keep them in alignment and something was going on that he didn't understand. They told me that since they moved into their new house, they had both been on edge and unable to hold adjustments. I suggested ECE, a house clearing, might be in order.

They had time and so did I that day. Their house was a large beautiful one-story Tuscan-Arizona style home. The house was only a few years old and despite its large windows and cathedral ceilings, it felt like walking into a cave. It gave me the impression of being closed in, dark and somewhat foreboding. Their black Labrador retriever was skulking on the other side of the room looking at me suspiciously with his head down, eyes up and a big sway in his back. He was not coming over to me at all. Unusual behavior for a Lab.

I turned within and asked what was going on. An image formed of small monkey like creatures that could move on two legs or four. They had prehensile tails and one of them was deeply embedded in the dogs back looking at me with its tail whipping in the air. Internally, I asked where the creatures had come from and was told there was a portal open in the fireplace. I used techniques I had been taught to secure the portal and to get these creatures to go back through to their dimension, time and place. The room was full of them and as I followed directions, they started clearing out.

As soon as one of them left the dog's back, the dog came over bright-eyed, without a sway in her back, and licked my feet. I extended the search for these creatures to the neighborhood which was also full of them. I called to them to come home and finally extended it throughout the world. These entities had been making mischief all over the planet. I stayed with it until the last of them disappeared into their own dimension and made sure they could not come back through.

The woman said her back felt better and her daughter came over and hugged her mother to her mother's surprise. The daughter had been moody, angry and generally difficult since they moved into this house. Her appearance had changed in the hour or so that I had been working on the house. I did a general clearing and a blessing and the house felt big, beautiful and bright. The cave-like feeling had disappeared.

After I explained what I had experienced, the woman told me the previous owner was an older woman who everyone in the neighborhood thought was crazy. She used to complain that she didn't get any sleep because of the guys dancing upstairs when there was no upstairs. She told stories of strange creatures that would keep her awake in the night.

I nodded and gave her my card telling her,

"They will not be bothering you anymore and if for some chance they do, call me."

She happily paid me and gave me a big heartfelt hug. I was delighted at being able to serve.

I continued to see the chiropractor and it seemed hopeful that perhaps we would move into a working relationship. One day in his waiting room a woman came in and almost fell on the floor trying to sit down. I rushed to her side out of concern, helped her to a seated position and asked if she would like me to run energy on her. With her consent I did and she started feeling better. She was walking better when she was taken into the chiropractor next as she was an emergency but when the chiropractor invited me into his office after seeing her, he read me the riot act. Who was I to think I could do something for one of his clients? He was quite angry and upset. I suspected the upset really didn't have that much to do with me but it was enough of an outburst that my hopes for a functional working relationship died.

Two weeks later I had a referral and did a house clearing for an old and large home. It was a home you could get lost in. It took several visits to even begin to feel like the home was clearing. I called Maria to ask if she would like to help. She did join me on one of the excursions and it felt powerful to have two of us working together. Unfortunately, that was the only other paying house clearing that I got in this area. So regular work in the desert was still evading me.

Chapter Twenty-Nine
Flipping

"Hello, Maria how are you?"

"Are you in or out?"

"In or out of what? What are you talking about? Slow down please."

"In or out of the renovations?" she continued with the same intensity.

"What are you talking about?"

Maria was a good friend who I had met in North Carolina. She started as a client, became a student, graduated and is a friend and partner in Earth healing. She had recently moved into the south end of the Phoenix valley.

She went on to explain she was working with a real estate agent who specialized in helping people buy houses to flip. She had an option on a repo house and she had to get her bid in today if she was going to do it. She wanted to know if we were in or out -- if we were going to work with her or not. We had only briefly talked about it and I didn't realize it was going to manifest this quickly. Maria's voice was tense.

"Hold on," I requested.

"Marc," I called to the other room. "Maria's on the phone and she wants to know if we're going to work with her on renovating houses."

"Well, neither one of us have found other work, so it seems like a good thing to try but let's ask if it's right action."

We both asked separately if it was right action and both got a strong 'yes' and returning to the phone I simply said,

"We're in!!!"

"OK," was Maria's response. "I'll place the bid." She hung up abruptly. She did not seem totally comfortable with this move but she also got that it was right action. So she courageously placed the bid.

It was only a couple of days later that Maria called and said that we had the house in a recently competed subdivision in Apache Junction, the easternmost part of the Valley.

With government repos you don't get to go inside until you have won the bid. It was a beautiful two-story Desert Tuscan style that was only a couple of years old. Inside it was a case of 'housal' abuse. The realtor had explained that when people knew they were losing their home, they sometimes took it out on the house and this was one of those times.

One of the kitchen cabinets had been punched through. Maria was figuring out how much it would take to replace all the cabinets.

"No, I can repair that and make it like new," I said confidently.

"Are you serious?"

"Yes, that's not a problem, the rest of the cabinets will clean up nicely."

"That will save us thousands of dollars and hours of work! But can you really do it?"

"Yes, I can. Well, I do want to earn my keep in this partnership."

I was grateful for the days working in the West Virginia dulcimer shop with Charles where I learned fine woodworking skills that would come in handy right now. We continued through the house. There were holes punched in some of the walls. Crayons and permanent markers marred the walls all over the house, so we would have to repaint the entire place. A library off the front door could be transformed into a bedroom with the addition of a closet and a door, increasing the value of the house significantly. We made plans and started our treks to and from Lowe's and Home Depot and got to work.

The three of us did a clearing ceremony on the first floor together asking for angelic and earth spirit assistance in healing the angry energies that filled the walls. When I went upstairs alone, I noticed curved red lines at head height in the master bath and I wondered what those were from. These were not crayon marks from the children. Internally I asked. A holographic image appeared of a man smashing a woman's head against the wall and blood spurting out.

"MARC!!!!!!!!!!! MARIA!!!!!!!!!!! I need you both up here now! We need to clear!"

Maria and Marc came up quickly and I explained what I had seen. They could both feel the negative energy in the room. We opened sacred space and started the process of another clearing ceremony. Once we were done, the energy felt completely different and I was calmer. We decided to clear each room. I used the rattle with high vibration crystals and Marc and Maria used chimes and a Tibetan bowl to vibrate the lower frequencies out of the structure. Afterwards, working in the house was much easier.

I started in on the cabinets and Marc worked on the transformation of the library. Both projects progressed well. Maria worked full time so she came after work and on weekends. When the repairs were completed we bought a large box of specialty cleaners to remove the children's marks - which never completely disappeared. A good primer and paint covered them completely. A neutral beige tone fit the style of the house well. Maria headed the spraying operation.

Something didn't feel right and the house did not sell the first day, so we performed a ceremony outside and sat in meditation asking what was going on. We were contacted eventually by some Native Americans who were concerned about the amount of building in the area. They told us of a sacred area on a mesa across the way and we assured them that laws had been passed so there would be no further building on the hills in this area. They seemed appeased and we were then able to shift the energy in the community. We started getting offers immediately and sold it at a good profit within a few days.

The next house was as far West as you could go in the Valley. A beautiful house that had little wrong with it but the things that were wrong were tricky. It was in a community with a restrictive HOA and the first week we received a $25 fine for having a few weeds in our stone front yard. What a nice welcome wagon.

I was the finish person for the walls on this house. The paints were all high end but each room had some problems. We didn't want to have to repaint the whole house. The main feature wall in the living room was two stories tall and a gray that nobody was able to match. I sat down and meditated asking what I should do with this wall. As I meditated a new experience occurred. It was like someone had a photograph that they brought into my head and through my eyes and I saw how the wall would look when complete. I had a lot of experience with specialty painting techniques over the years including helping to create the beautiful walls at Waldorf Schools.

"I'm going to the store now. I know what to do," I yelled over my shoulder.

"What are you doing? Are you sure you know what you're doing?" Maria once again did not have experience with my skills and was understandably skeptical but I was insistent that I knew what to do.

"I'll have it done tonight you'll see it'll be spectacular, not just good," but I could feel her continued concern. "And if you don't like it, we will have time to paint over it."

At Lowe's I had no difficulty finding the right materials. I chose my paints according to the image quite vivid in my memory. I painted a silver color and then a shiny white over the matte gray using a roller sponge. In the end, it looked like you were looking into a starry night! It made the room look twice as big. It was an amazing optical illusion that showed how different paint can make the perception of a room. We all stared at the wall and agreed it was spectacular. It didn't look sponged. It looked like expensive wallpaper or a custom paint job an artist had spent weeks painting. It fit perfectly with the house and no trace of the former irregularities showed.

This process repeated itself several times. The house had a hallway that was two stories tall and way out of proportion. I felt like Alice in Wonderland wandering through a giant's hallway. I meditated there looking for an answer. The paint was great but marred in a few places. I asked how to do this and again a vision came through me and applied itself to the wall; I saw exactly how it was supposed to be.

"Marc can you figure out the Fibonacci sequence for putting stripes on this wall?" He was happy to oblige but questioned my design decision.

I convinced both Marc and Maria to let me try and we painted two stripes on the wall one larger than the other according to the Fibonacci sequence leaving the wall color as a stripe between. It completely changed the perception of the proportions of the hallway making it appear human-sized again. We all walked through the hallway repeatedly just to observe how effective this optical illusion was.

It was time for me to go back to North Carolina and we only had one day to go before I left, I thought we were done but Maria pointed out a place in the dining room where the paint had buckled. She touched it and the paint peeled off making a large space in a burnt orange feature wall. Now familiar with the process, I sat in meditation asking how do we work with this wall? A vision popped through. Gold and brown paint and the right sponge for the task worked. I felt Marc watching me work for a time.

"It's fractals," he said thoughtfully. "The placement needs to be random but the pattern is the same," he analyzed what I was doing in his intellectual way.

When I finished with the wall the same day it looked like high-end wallpaper, making it a real feature wall. It also toned down the strong color making the room appear larger. We were all pleased and relieved and I was able to leave for North Carolina on time. The house sold in two days.

When Maria first came to Arizona, she moved into a house in the far South of the Phoenix Valley. The apartment we started in was central to the Valley, the house we moved to was in the North. The first flipper house was in the East, the next West. We blessed each house as we completed the repairs and did a ceremony asking for the right people to buy the house. When we completed the last house, I had a vision of a Native American dancing and got the idea we had just created a medicine wheel around the entire Phoenix Valley.

"*Wow*," I thought, "*You don't have to know what you are doing; you just have to follow your guidance step by step and if you are fortunate, you'll understand the why and see the bigger picture in the end.*"

Chapter Thirty
Bliss & Ecstasy

On a return trip to North Carolina, I participated in a La Ho Chi training facilitated by Dan and Rio Watson in Hillsborough, NC. La Ho Chi is an energy healing system. I had taken the basic trainings and was now an assistant. Assistants helped in the first part and were given a time to have our own session later in the workshop. During mine, I was taken to a Chamber of bliss and ecstasy. It was…well how do I describe it? It was joy and way beyond joy. It was contentment, it was home, it was where I wanted to be forever. It was amazing – actually, it was so amazing that I didn't want to come back. My healing partner tried to bring me back in the gentle method prescribed by the training to no avail. I could hear her but I wasn't interested. I kept thinking in my head, "*I'm not coming back, this is where I want to stay, this is where I want to live, this is where I belong and this is my home.*" She got Rio who kept shaking me and loudly saying,

"Lyneah!!! You have to come back!!!!!!!!" She grabbed pictures of Sedona, telling me how beautiful it was there and how Marc was waiting for me and I just kept feeling inside myself,

"*Go away, I am not coming back.*" I think she sensed this and started shaking a little harder. I don't think Rio was interested in having someone die on her table during her class. I could understand. I just wasn't interested.

The pair next to us had already traded places. The woman who was now on the table was having what they call an 'accelerated healing' experience. She was crying and fussing and making lots of noise. Clearly, she was in a great deal of emotional pain. I could feel her anguish.

"*As long as there are people in pain I'm going to have to come back,*" I thought and I did, albeit reluctantly.

121

On my next trip back to North Carolina, Rio had organized a healing class with Flo Magdalena, an internationally known healer and author and it promised to be intense. Each person in the limited-sized group would have one session with all the other women working on her. There were nine of us, all advanced healers. I set my intention to go to the room of bliss and ecstasy again and in my session, I got to the door quickly. Two strong angelic presences guarded the entry to the cave with spears that were crossed blocking the opening. I looked at them and I said,

"*I promise I'll go back; I just need to come in for a little while to get my fix.*" I continued to beg and plead.

They had absolutely no sense of humor and did not change their Marine-like stances. Nor did they yield the spears. The message came not from these two beings but from my guides: "*You must learn to ground bliss and ecstasy on the Earth with your partner Marc. You will not be allowed entry here.*"

"*Ever????*" I asked. There was no response. I was upset but understood. I asked what I was supposed to work on today and shifted into some energies I needed to release. Everyone in the group received major healings that day.

Talking with Marc later, I said,

"We have to ground bliss and ecstasy."

"Oh, gee, darn but somebody has to do it," was his response.

Back in the workshop Flo explained about the bandage around her thumb,

"I knew it was going to happen. It was just something I had to go through. I just cut the thumb off with an axe."

I knew that feeling. I had it when the logging incident happened. I didn't know why at the time but I had a feeling it was something I had to go through. I worked on her healing thumb during breaks and felt a good connection with Flo.

Some months later I called Flo to ask her something and she said, "Did you say you are in North Carolina?"

"Yes." I answered.

"Oh, you have to meet this person who did healing work on my thumb. She's the real deal. She helped it heal much faster. I can't remember her name but she was at the women's workshop. Rio can tell you who she is."

"Was her name possibly Lyneah?" I asked.

"Yes, it was. Do you know her?"

"That would be me." I smiled internally. Hearing this from such a powerful healer brought me great waves of joy.

Chapter Thirty-One
Mysterious Disappearances

Arizona is full of interesting stories. Salty old miner types, rockhounds abound, leaver rocks. I took a lapidary class at the Arizona Mining and Mineral Museum and learned to cut and polish semi-precious stones. I have one flat cabochon from that class which is precious to me. The gentleman who ran the shop, Duffy, was a sweet slightly salty miner type and he often regaled us with his tales. One day I brought a stone in that I found on a hike.

"Oh, that's a leaver rock," he said seriously looking at me for a response.

"What's a leaver rock?" I asked.

"When you find it, you leave 'er right there."

We all had a good laugh.

The shop usually had a stone of some sort on the machine that created smooth round spheres. It was fascinating to watch. One day a discussion arose over Montezuma's Well. It is a Native site containing cliff dwellings and sophisticated irrigation systems. The well-constructed place supported 60 acres of agriculture from the spring fed well which functions even in drought conditions in the desert.

We went to visit this impressive site. All this was suddenly abandoned and no one knows why. The water in the lake, around which the cliff dwellings were constructed, had become poisoned with arsenic and only five species of creatures adapted to this condition. As we walked around admiring the ingenuity that went into constructing this amazing place, which had been a green thriving oasis, I wondered: what happened? No one really knows.

* * * * *

The day of the Superbowl, I had an appointment at the Enlightenment Center early enough for me to avoid the game traffic. On my way home, however, I went way out of my way to avoid the area but ended up in a parking lot across the highway from the spaceship-like dome. I turned the car off and asked,

"Why am I here?"

A picture unfolded. The game had already started and I could feel the excitement rising from over here. With my internal sight I was shown a huge ball of energy building.

"Harness this energy. The angels will take it at your request and store it for times when it is needed. Right now, it radiates without purpose. You can give it purpose with your request. Angels cannot violate free will, so your request will give them permission."

* * * * *

I was referred to another place in Ahwatukee, southeast of Phoenix. This was a rather exotic store that also had a room for energy work and space for psychic readings. I do not consider myself psychic, I much prefer the word intuitive. I went there to see about teaching classes, doing meditations and energy work. The store had an Egyptian theme, the owner was an elegant German woman. I worked there for some time before customers kept pressuring her to have a reader. She asked me several times and finally I said I would try.

The first woman who came for a reading was one who basically wanted permission to have an affair. I went into meditation and found that she had previously cheated on her husband in a past life and this time was for her to redeem herself and not give in. She didn't like that at all. I was intuitive enough to know what she wanted from me and ethical enough not to give it to her. A few people really wanted to know tendencies and energies around the current life situation but most wanted to be validated in what they already had decided to do. I stopped readings not long after beginning them.

We had some lovely classes and meditations and met some interesting people at this store. One was a woman who came for energy healing, then meditations, then classes. She always had a skeptical edge but kept showing up and showing interest.

One day after class she remained.

"I'd like to hire you to come up to my cabin in Oak Creek Canyon to do a clearing."

"OK, when?"

We discussed the details and set the date. I arrived at the huge 'cabin'. It was a log home probably around 3000 square feet. Her husband was a medical doctor and when I arrived, I saw two Native American spirits sitting in the rocking chairs on the porch. A woman came out and told me not to sit in the rocking chairs. I said I understood why. She appeared to have been drinking. She disappeared and I never saw her again while I was there.

The doctor husband greeted me while watching a March Madness game. His wife asked me to help him feel comfortable with my presence. Not sure, I opened to guidance. The Mountaineers (go 'eers) were doing quite well that year. I watched the game the previous night with interest. I am not the kind of person who can generally quote any kind of sports data but I had a detailed conversation with this man talking about specific players and the moves they made. The whole game was showing up in my imagination as it had been played. Not a usual skill for me! That impressed him.

"Yeah, nice to meet you. Go, work with my wife and do whatever you need to do," and he went back to his game. That was the last I saw of him.

"We have to meditate and each get the story first. Then you will tell me what you get," she directed in her skeptical way. We sat on benches near the occupied rockers.

"It should be a happy place. It is gorgeous and it's in a beautiful wood near the river and all I can do is cry."

I could see by the red in her eyes that she had done her fair share of crying today.

We sat outside in meditation. After some time of quiet I heard the chief say,

"*Metal spiders out of the sky, fire out of their bellies,*" and I saw an image of many Native Americans running in shock and turmoil while spaceships with long metal legs pursued them killing them with laser rays out of the bottom of the ships. It was like a page out of a Marvel comic book. I had done some research and this was another of those people disappeared places in Arizona. Previously a tribe of 1,000 Native people lived in this river valley. They had mysteriously disappeared leaving artifacts behind. This message, although surprising, fit.

I opened my eyes and shortly thereafter she opened hers. She looked at me in a challenging way and asked what I got. I told her what the chief said and her eyes widened. She had gotten different words but basically the same message we had both seen hundreds and hundreds of people mowed down in the prime of their lives. I could see the chief nodding his head as he rocked in the chair on the porch. Another man, his son occupied the second chair.

"What now?" she asked.

I guided all of us through a ceremony including the process of helping these souls cross over. It took a couple of hours for all of them to go, especially some that tried to evade us. The chief was last and made sure all went through before he said his thanks and disappeared into the light.

Spent and mind blown, I walked down to the river to put my feet in. Before I got to the river, I felt blocked by the energy of tall spirits. I asked who was there and was told Metatron and two Hathors. I communed with them for a time, then cooled my feet in the chilly waters of Oak Creek contemplating, as Douglas Adams would have said, "Life, the Universe and Everything."

The woman later reported that she had no more tears at the cabin. She never, however, lost her edge of skepticism, which is a good thing. William Bengtson[3] says a skeptic is someone who neither believes nor disbelieves. He says he'd rather work with a skeptic any day over believers or non-believers. His story of how he became involved in energy healing is a good one. He was a major

---

[3] See *The Energy Cure* and *Hands On Healing* by William Bengtson.

skeptic himself and was tricked into the initial research he had come to observe.

Chapter Thirty-Two
Manifesting Smooth Air

"I am a Lieutenant, an M.D. and a pilot in the Luftwaffe", reported Luke in his German accented English.

"Do you mean Lufthansa?" I asked, feeling confused.

"No, Luftwaffe," he said with upright posture and bright blue eyes.

"German Air Force? Where?" I asked, expecting to hear some German city's name.

"Right here in Goodyear, Arizona."

"You mean to tell me there's a German Air Force base in the United States?"

"That's exactly what I'm telling you and I am stationed at it."

Surprised, I stared, having nothing to say. Luke and Marc and I became good friends. Luke once had a healing crisis that Western medicine was unable to touch. Energy healing introduced him to integrative health care. It changed his life. We had good conversations at the Enlightenment Center. Luke felt like a long lost good brother. Luke's wife was a talented painter and I still have her painting of a violet flame angel.

*****

On my way to a healer's group at the Enlightenment Center, I started feeling the unmistakable pain of a kidney stone. The pain steadily increased and I asked,

"Am I to go home?"

"No."

"Am I to continue to the center?"

"Yes."

So, I drove there. Luke was the first person I saw. I was bent over with the pain.

"I need help passing a kidney stone," I informed him flatly.

"Do you mean you need to be taken to the hospital?" his medical mind jumped in.

"No, we can heal it together here," I assured him. With concern, he quickly brought me into an empty treatment room, asked someone to gather the other healers, helped me lie down on the table. There were thirteen of us in that room and I co-directed things from on the table. Luke examined me in his doctor's way and confirmed that it was indeed a kidney stone. We quickly discussed what to do. As the healers came in each started running energy in his or her way. When everyone was in place, I suggested,

"Get a picture of the stone in your mind and we will all together break it up energetically. When you have the picture well in mind, we will all clap at the same time intending the stone to break up easily without pain please," I was fighting to overcome the pain, which was somewhere near a 12 on a ten-point scale.

Luke took over and helped everyone focus on the stone, which allowed me to relax. When the clap happened, the pain disappeared instantly. After is was clear I was fine, a relieved Luke confessed,

"You taught me a lot today." Despite all his accomplishments in life he was still a humble man, which one could miss if you didn't see through his upright posture and tough Luftwaffe Germanic exterior.

*****

One day Luke asked,

"Would you like to go flying with me?"

"Of course," I said quickly and added, "but does the Luftwaffe allow that?"

"No, not with the Luftwaffe, with me in my Piper Cub. I am part of a co-op that jointly owns a plane and I will reserve it for us." Marc and I enthusiastically nodded yes.

We made the arrangements and the day we arrived at the small private airfield it was sunny but windy. Marc got into the back seat and I took the co-pilot's chair.

"I will take off but after we are in the air you can take over and fly if you would like." Luke said to me knowing my interest and love of flying. I had flown a small plane twice before and wanted to take lessons but budget and location had not offered an easy option so far.

After a smooth take off, we were in the air but it was quite bumpy. Luke explained that there were many air currents today and that it would be a bumpy ride. He turned to me asking if I would like to take over the controls. My smile gave him a big yes and I was soon holding the co-pilot's wheel. In a few minutes, the turbulence ceased and I relaxed more, feeling more comfortable handling the plane. Luke looked at me strangely with an unexpressed question. He looked at Marc in the back seat then he looked forward and then at me again. Something was bothering him but I was reasonably sure it wasn't my flying which was joyful and going smoothly. After a time of contemplation and questioning he said,

"She's manifesting smooth air!!!!!!!"

I didn't think that was possible but when he named it, I realized I had been putting out an energy from my will forces and my solar plexus chakra that smoothed the air. It was an unconscious act. Now conscious of it, I was able to continue manifesting and we had a smooth ride the rest of the way.

"I didn't think that possible." I spoke aloud.

"Neither did I." Luke confessed. "I've never experienced such a thing before. When you took over the wheel, it was not long before the bumpiness stopped. I was confused because all the weather indications said we would have turbulence all day over the entire valley, so I started asking what had happened and I intuitively got that you were doing it. I asked how and was told you were manifesting smooth air."

"She can be a rather surprising person," added Marc from the back seat.

I flew the rest of the trip and continued to manifest smooth air. We had a delightfully smooth ride and when it came time to landing, Luke informed me,

"You are going to land the plane."

"Oh, I don't know about that. I don't think I am ready," I said with apprehension. Flying is one thing, landing another - and I had not tried it before.

"You can do it. I'll be right here helping. I'm your back up person," encouraged Luke. Marc in the back seat was silent.

"OK, I'll try."

"You will do it," corrected Luke. I nodded tentatively.

The landing was an amazing high. Marc's Uncle Manny, a former Navy pilot, used to say,

"Flying is the second greatest thrill to mankind. Landing is the first."

The next time I flew to North Carolina, the flight had turbulence. I wondered,

"Could it work on a commercial jet?"

I started doing what I did in the Piper Cub consciously. It took major effort but I did manage to smooth things out.

"Did I really do that or was that just a coincidence?" I wondered. I let go of the energy I was producing and we went back into turbulence in a short time. Again, I produced the smooth air energy and the shaking stopped. Air travel has been seriously more comfortable since.

"What else can we do that no one told us we could do?" I wondered.

Chapter Thirty-Three
A New School of Healing

When you can't find work, give it away. That is based on the idea that what you need more of, give, and it has worked in my life. I had been a hospice volunteer for many years in North Carolina. After contacting a few hospice services in the Phoenix Valley, I chose one. I helped with training, families and hospice patients. I met interesting people in the process and found it fulfilling.

It worked. Although I was giving my services in one direction, clients appeared from another but this time it was not a flood, it was more like a drizzle.

One of my new clients was a professional woman who led a large division of a company. She was friendly but also formal. She was almost 6 feet tall. I did not know her well. She came to the house as I had a treatment room now that our border had moved out. She wanted to know what direction she should take next in her life. She was searching for her purpose, despite her apparent success in the business world. She laid fully clothed face up on the table and I started running energy at her ears. The ears contain terminals for all the meridians in the body, so if you are aware of energy flow you can work on the entire body from the ears.

I did my opening and asked for the guides that were optimal to work with us that day. I felt Saint Germain's presence strongly. I could feel that her spine was quite out of alignment, her body twisted and uncomfortable.

"Tell her she needs a new attitude," I heard Saint Germain say.

"You need a new attitude," I informed her.

"What attitude would that be?" she asked.

In my mind I opened for the answer. After a pause, I heard two clear words,

"*Fuck it.*"

"*What???*" I screamed internally. "*I can't say that to this woman, I barely know her and she's a professional and proper and…*" I protested in my head.

"*Say it! Say it! Say it!*" I heard all too clearly.

"Yes…" she prompted expectantly. She was waiting for a few drops of wisdom and I didn't think I had any. I took a deep breath, waited for something else to come into my consciousness and heard,

"*Say it! Say it! Say it!*"

"Seriously?" I asked.

"*Say it! Say it! Say it!*"

Finally, I reluctantly gave in.

"Your new attitude is…" I began.

"Yes. I'm ready," she responded.

"Your new attitude is…..Fuck It!"

An explosion of laughter rocked her body and her spine adjusted and the twist straightened as she shook the table with laughter that went on for minutes while peals of tension released from her body. I could still feel Saint Germain's laughter and his attitude of 'see I told you it would work.' He was stepping aside and Mother Mary became our next guide. She directed me to put loving energy into the spaces where my client released waves of tension and stress.

When she finally stopped the strong laughter, a beautiful smile appeared on her face. Her whole body was as relaxed as if she had received an hour and a half hot stone massage.

In teaching healing classes, I tell this story to encourage students to listen to their guidance even when it is not comfortable or what you expect. Make sure only benevolent beings are present who are right action to work with you and have your highest good at heart from Divine Source's point of view, then trust.

The story is usually received with much laughter and more than one student has recommended I start a new healing program called 'Fuck It Therapy'. To date, I have resisted but the memory gives me great joy and laughter. There is great joy in following guidance and watching it blossom.

Chapter Thirty-Four
The North Rim

Marc and I drove to the Grand Canyon North Rim admiring the views the entire way. We checked into our adorable rustic little cabin and settled in. It included a kitchen, a small table, a bathroom, a bed and a front porch with rocking chairs. All we needed. By now I had been to the Grand Canyon many times but this was my first experience of the generally less-visited north side. I had expected it to be less populated but it was full of people.

After dinner we watched the sun go down from the comfort of the rocking chairs. The sun set made extreme shadows in the Canyon. It was a cloudless night, dark of the moon and we expected to see a wonderful display of stars. What we were not expecting was a wide array of telescopes. An astronomy group was here for what was known as some of the best viewing of the year. People put papers on their telescopes indicating which planet, moon or galaxy they had zeroed in on and they were proud to share. Many had hi-tech tracking and high magnification scopes. When it was fully dark, we started to make the rounds peering through each telescope gasping at the beauty we were able to see. Later, staring out over the canyon into the night sky made me think of Carl Sagan talking about billions and billions of stars. Here this didn't feel like an exaggeration. I wondered what it had been like in earlier days with less light and fewer forms of pollution to block the stars.

There's something about staring into a star-filled sky that floods my soul with joy. I think fondly of my mother whenever I see Cassiopeia, her favorite constellation and silently thank her for sharing starry nights with me in Wisconsin as we sat in chaise lounges for hours staring up at the stars. She taught me the major constellations and taught me the power of just staring into the night sky. The Milky Way shown beautifully over our driveway. I've been told staring into a full stary night sky activates spiritual centers in the brain. Here there were so many stars it was difficult to pick out the Milky Way. The North Rim was a most memorable and excellent early birthday present from Marc.

If you live in the city and don't have easy access to the stars, you can use a piece of goldstone as a gazing ball. They come in blue (purple), green and gold. The purple is my favorite and I have a necklace with a large bead of purple goldstone on it.

This trip was planned in between house flips, so we didn't have a great deal of time. We had to get back to work again. We felt strongly guided where to go but we didn't know the why. We drove through Kanab, Utah, turned right and headed for Lake Powell. On the way we stopped at a place that was calling to us; it had nothing obvious by sight, nothing special in terms of the geology, certainly no signs of civilization. We both felt strongly we had to stop here. We walked as we were guided to a place a short way off the road in an open flat area surrounded by rocks. Marc held space, creating a strong field of safety in which to work. In deep meditation, I started to see a Native American man's spirit wrapped in a shroud of energy. He seemed trapped, imprisoned in this energy slowly rotating in place. Getting that this was why we were here, I asked for directions on what to do. Following the intuitive directions, I unwound the energy and started to lift him out. Three very tall spirits came and said they would take him to a rehab place and I asked my guides if they were here for the highest good and got a resounding '*yes*'. I handed him softly over to these gentle giants, who were around 20 feet tall. Before he left, the newly freed spirit weakly raised one hand and pointed in a direction which we followed. We found many animal spirits also shrouded in similar energy fields. We gently removed each and angels came to take them across into the golden portal of light which had opened for their benefit. This process took a long time. It felt so right to do. We felt great joy and gratitude to be of service in this amazing way. Now I understood why we were not told why we were coming here. As with so many other times, I probably would have said,

"You need a different person, one more qualified. I can't do that (open a portal, stop an earthquake, rescue tortured souls), I don't live in a science fiction movie" -- or do I?

Much later, a friend's teenage daughter asked me to go with her to see a *Harry Potter* movie. I was interested in what all the buzz was about. The movie opened with an image of a person revolving above a table entrapped in a cloud of energy. I was shocked at how closely it paralleled that day's vision.

* * * * *

Lake Powell was an oasis in the long expanses of desert and sparse grazing lands. The beautiful deep blue of the water was soothing to my eyes. Giant banded red, white and pink sandstone sculptures carved by water, banked the shores. This man-made (by Glen Canyon Dam) reservoir on the Colorado River spans between Utah and Arizona. The lake is 185 miles long and covers an area of 254 square miles, second in the U.S. only to Lake Mead at Las Vegas. Along the curves the rocks were sculpted into many different formations, some smooth and sloping giving colored concentric circles, others sharp-edged making dramatic dives into the water. The sun was bright and intense and the sky not quite as deep a blue as the water. I would have gladly stayed here a month or more volunteering as a trash picker for the park, swimming, enjoying other water sports and hiking. Maybe someday. This trip it was only a few quick stops and not even one to swim.

We overnighted at Bluff, again enjoying the food and the energy. The energy between us was good even in this concentrated traveling style. We 'ooed' and 'ahhhed' at the beautiful sandstone sculptures of Arches National Monument. Moab, another oasis in Utah, was lunch. Restaurants catered to the healthy type and I easily found delicacies on the menu. Procuring directions to a swimming hole along one of the rivers, I talked Marc into changing into bathing trunks, I was already in my bathing suit. We walked over beautiful red rocks to a widening in the river where we spent the afternoon cooling in the delicious waters.

We followed the Colorado River through an impressive canyon to Grand Junction. Our next destination was Silverton, Colorado. The road there is US 550 and it's called the Million Dollar highway.

"The amazing thing is that it's here at all," said Marc. "A massive project to build,"

"It's a difficult road to drive, especially from my side where there are no guardrails and the drop is oooooh probably 5000 feet!"

Progress was slow, studded with many switchbacks and I was grateful there was no snow on the road as we climbed higher and higher. Silverton is at an elevation of 9,318 ft. When you could look out the views were magnificent. I often found myself focused on the road believing four eyes were safer than two in this situation. Some of the time I had to drive to keep from getting motion sickness. When we left Phoenix, it was 105° F; when we got to Silverton it was snowing in August!

The silver mines were no longer working. Mining trails still streamed down the steep slopes and we wondered if we could find some silver. No such luck. We did find one mine open to tour.

Lighted miner's hard hats atop our heads, we ducked into one of the open cars. There were few people on this tour but I could feel many more spirits in the mine. When we came out, our car had hitchhikers. We took time to listen to the spirit's stories of mining collapses and injuries that had caused death. We helped each one cross over after listening to his tale. There were no women. After this clearing, the atmosphere still didn't seem right. Checking into our hotel room, we finally had cell phone reception and many messages. We worked with a team of earth healers who came together for various purposes. One was lessening the severity or changing the direction of hurricanes. The messages informed us of Katrina. It was August 28, 2005. We had not had television nor cell coverage for several days and were quite out of touch with the news.

In meditation we were immediately told not to do anything to ameliorate this storm. I checked that I was centered and aligned and hearing divine truth. The message was the same. Marc provided confirmation. I called Joe and he told us he had the same message. He reported,

"I don't understand it either, it's a big storm, supposed to hit at Category Five. We can send healing energy to those who are in its path but we are not to reduce nor redirect this storm. It is needed for some reason. I've called the entire team and we all get this message."

I was stunned. We had been entirely out of touch but now we watched the storm and its path. People were evacuating the Louisiana coast but there were many who had no means to leave. We started praying and doing energy work as guided.

In the morning we drove South to Durango, a cowboy and artist town I was surprised Marc liked. He suggested a potential move there. We looked for work but found no leads. It was a pleasant town, not too big but large enough to have what you needed. It was a gentler terrain than the northern part of Colorado and a milder climate but I felt no energy to move there.

West from Durango after a delicious lunch, the cliff dwellings of Mesa Verde called loudly to us. The Anasazi Natives, known as the Pueblo people, lived in the cliff villages constructed in the 13th Century. Less than one mile into the park, we were in a traffic jam inching down the road behind a long line of cars. At a bend in the road, we could see why: a road crew was marking the center line and would not allow anyone to pass. It would take hours to get to the Cliff dwellings which were many miles into the park.

We asked if there was a place along the way that might do. We got an indication to turn on a side road, found a small parking space and one bench overlooking a beautiful view. We sat for some time meditating and listening. As if out of a mist, the very tall Native Americans who had appeared in Utah to rescue the entrapped man formed in front of us. They bowed their heads in respect and said,

"Thank you so much for your work. We have waited a long time for someone to come and help us. We were unable to do this ourselves because it required someone in third dimension who could break the spell. The man you rescued was a strong, powerful shaman who was tricked by a sorceress who wanted his power. She managed to trap him. The sorceress was also responsible for the animals that you freed. Now that she no longer has their power,

143

it is likely she will have to leave her physical body. She was living on their stolen energy."

Tears were streaming down my face as they explained. I was not accustomed to being recognized for this kind of work or having such explanations and verification. It is something I do as a service and did not talk about very much at that time. The energy of their gratitude was overwhelming. They continued,

"There will be a gift waiting for you. It is something you have long desired and it will now be made available for you. It is one way that we can thank you. Know you have our deepest gratitude. Think of us. We remain ever grateful. Our shaman friend is doing well in recovery. He sends his gratitude though he is not yet able to travel. Continue your work, it is important and there are currently not enough willing to follow such guidance at this time. Your work is making a difference in the world. A bigger difference than you know. Be encouraged."

They walked off into the distance. I was impressed and surprised at the clarity of their communications. I felt the energy of their gratitude like a warm blanket around me. Tears of overwhelm continued to stream down my face. Marc teared up as well and put a tender arm around me and held me for a time. Then he guided me to the car and we were both silent needing to process. It was miles before the tears stopped for me.

We passed through Cortez and into Holbrook for the night. I was getting ready for breakfast when I had ideas coming into my mind saying negative things about Marc, trying to get me to be angry with him. *"That's not how I feel,"* I thought and asked where these ideas were coming from. In meditation I was shown entities. I asked what to do and was told to imagine placing them in blue jars on a metaphysical shelf. That worked and the foreign thoughts left.

From Holbrook we drove to Show Low and South through the Salt River Canyon, a 32,000-acre wilderness. Here the rocks were various shades of brown and studded with green trees, bushes and mosses. It was refreshing to see so much green. We came to Theodore Roosevelt Lake, a large reservoir. Marc knew my love of water, so he had planned water into this trip and I was grateful. Another stunning set of landscapes filled my soul with their haunting beauty but no time to stop for a swim. He understood my need for water but did not yet understand my need included submersing myself for long periods of time. He describes himself as rather cat-like when it comes to water.

Back though Chandler and into Phoenix to compete this trip, my body was road weary. Marc seemed to be energized by constant driving. I was drained by it. I felt like the Sherpas carrying supplies for a group climbing Mount Everest. They were making good time and stopped for a break. The leaders pointed out how far they had come in a short time and the Sherpas sat refusing to go further. The man who translated for them asked why. The Sherpas responded that they had to wait for their spirits to catch up with them.

When I laid down to sleep that night my eyes were filled with the beauty of the many landscapes. I was overloaded with the magnificence of Mother Earth and impressed with the differences between one area to the next. I needed time to process it all. Many places we stopped at deserved at least a week of exploration. Many of these landscapes brought old cowboy movies to life. So different from the East Coast, I now understood those from the West who had moved East having the major complaint,

"I need more space." If you grew up with these rambling vistas, nothing east of the Mississippi could satisfy your need for wide open spaces.

Marc and I had been compatible on this trip despite our differences in travel style. We had grown closer with the shared experiences and felt the sparkles between us growing that Valorie had mentioned. I appreciated Marc's stamina for driving. I appreciated the comfort of the silences between us and the times we took to meditate together. I was extremely grateful to be with someone who simply held space, supported me and didn't judge even when the experiences were pretty outrageous by normal standards. I offered a prayer of gratitude and felt great joy. I had been clear with spirit that I was ok being alone and that if I was to have a partner, it had to be a mutually supportive loving relationship in which both of us would be able to grow on our spiritual paths. I was beginning to feel I had found this.

Chapter Thirty-Five
Squash Blossom

I went to the computer and opened my email. One post lit up. When I say lit up, I mean it looked illuminated like the effect on the TV show *Touched by an Angel*. It felt like it was stretching out of the computer at me saying 'open me'. I opened it immediately, curious what was calling me. It was from Tom Kenyon asking for those who felt guided to come and help shift the Earth's timeline. I didn't know what that meant but I knew I had to go.

Later in the day I received emails from Maria and Cristina saying that they felt strongly guided to go as well. I signed up and planned the drive to Albuquerque. Marc did not feel guided to go and he brought up an issue that was a deal breaker for me. We had several deep conversations about it and had slept on the issue, I had stated my stance but he had priorities to consider and decisions to make. I felt it was good for us to be apart while he considered his side. It would be an adjustment to go our separate ways after the closeness we had achieved but I would do what I had to do to not lose myself again. This trip was a high priority. We parted on tenuous terms. I had made my position clear and now it was his turn to decide. I drove to Albuquerque trying to focus on admiring the landscape along the way and feeling the anticipation of seeing two good friends and accomplishing an amazing piece of earth healing work.

Maria, Cristina and I managed to get our rooms in the same part of the hotel. Settling in quickly, we went to dinner.

"Oh darlings, I'm so glad you made it," Virginia Essene hugged each one of us like we were her long lost children. We all felt the strong energetic connection. With little effort Virginia left a lasting impression.

147

"You must join us for dinner darlings, I'm so glad you are here; we're going to a fantastic Italian place..." and she herded us and a few others out the door and provided directions.

None of us had met Virginia before (at least not in this lifetime) but she said we had been her children in a previous lifetime and displayed an affection that made that feel entirely plausible. Dinner was filled with delightful, interesting conversations. Everyone here was metaphysical and some, like Virginia, had been for many decades.

That night Tom Kenyon started the workshop by telling us that the Hathors had asked him to do an additional workshop this month. His response was,

"Look at my calendar - there is no room."

They left because they are not imposing beings and later Judy, Tom's partner, asked him to go back to ask the Hathors what they wanted and why; she felt it was important.

"*Earth needs more time,*" was their response. "*In order for the shift to be less traumatic, there needs to be a shift in the timeline and you can do that with the group of people who will come.*"

This was the basis for the workshop; we were there to change time. Again, an assignment that I had no clue how to do. Most of the long weekend was spent in meditation listening to Tom play the crystal heart bowl with about 80 of us chanting to the four elements: El for Earth, Kah for Fire, Leem for Water and Om for Air. Between practice sessions, Tom told stories and introduced meditations familiar and new.

The breaks were like going to a museum with all the major crystal pieces people wore. I was standing in a group and began feeling my feet wanting to lift off the floor. I started to feel dizzy. I recognized this feeling: moldavite.

"I don't see any moldavite," I said to the group. One woman pulled a large chunk necklace of moldavite from under her sweater. It made me even dizzier. I felt my feet lifting off the floor.

"How can you wear that?" I asked.

"I am a triple Taurus. If I don't wear it, my feet are several inches under the ground."

"I'm sorry, I need to move away, it is making me dizzy." She replaced the necklace under her clothing which helped a little but I went to the bathroom to regain center and to ground myself again.

I called Marc and got his voice mail. I had spent some time reconsidering my decision which only reinforced my point of view. I wondered how he was doing in his considerations. I really enjoyed Marc's company and had come to have great respect for him and how kind he was but this issue was another deal breaker and I tried to tuck the apprehension I felt into my back pocket to be dealt with later. I needed to focus on this task at hand.

Tom told us about the special place being developed for an intentional community. Virginia Essene was one of the organizers. We would be bused to the location. Judy told the story of being instructed to create an acupuncture needle of sorts for the earth; they had a company come in and drill a 500-foot-deep hole which was then filled with pink and white quartz. It was intended to provide energy into the earth. Quite the endeavor, a drill rig and a truckload of crystals in a remote location. The man who headed up the drilling operation came to Judy after it was complete and expressed how proud he was that he had put a cap on the bottom. Judy was beside herself and told him he would have to take everything out, take the cap off and replace everything back with no cap on the bottom. He did so even though he didn't understand. Many of their stories made my Earth healing endeavors seem somewhat commonplace and minor in comparison even though I realized when we each do our part, the whole gets accomplished.

Perfect weather greeted us on the way to the site. Bright sunshine with a nice breeze made it comfortable. The buses were not able to go the whole way and we had a good walk. It was so nice to be with Maria and Cristina. We picked out our places to meditate. I found a spot under a small juniper tree, perfect for the four-hour meditation.

Tom and Judy called us all together at the monument built over the drilled crystal-filled shaft. A copper pyramid topped a four-foot brick cube. Each side had an altar honoring one of the four elements. We were asked to approach each element and leave our offerings: tobacco, flowers, crystals, grains and water. This was the first place I had been in the Southwest that you could not see even one telephone or electric line in any direction and the views were wide and long. It is a special place.

After the group gathering and offerings, we were sent off to do our meditations, silently appealing to all four elements. I settled in under my juniper tree and was happy to have a long time to meditate. Five minutes later, somebody poked me telling me it was time to come back. We weren't supposed to talk but I was so surprised that I said,

"It's not time yet."

The man looked at me without speaking and showed me his watch -- four hours had passed! I simply could not believe it, my inner sense said ten minutes max.

Regrouping around the altars, Tom explained the Hathors informed him that we had gotten the Earth more time for its transition to happen in a more peaceful way. I was glad to be part of this but everything inside me said I had been cheated out of a long meditation! I had to laugh at myself. Switching perspectives, I focused on how grateful I felt to be part of such an amazing event. My time sense confirmed that we had changed time.

I decided to stay in town another day based on my guidance. The AMTA (American Massage Therapy Association) Convention was going on at that time but I was guided not to go. I wandered around town not sure what I was supposed to do and found myself in Old Albuquerque. I had been here once many years ago. My at-that-time in-laws lived in the area and suggested that we go to the Indian center to see the dances. I wasn't really interested because I was afraid it was going to be some hokey thing for tourists but I went because it gave me a break from the in-laws. When the head male dancer of the Native American troupe came in, he stood for a long time waiting for attention and a shift in energy in the audience. He never spoke he didn't need to. He just held space strongly and gradually the voices silenced. He was well dressed and his fingers seemed covered in sea of perfectly clear blue princess turquoise. Bracelets and necklaces completed his outfit. He held a drum he only used during the dances. When he had everyone's attention he announced,

"We are not here to perform. We are here to share sacred dance." I could feel him clearing the area and elevating the energies. He was a strong presence. His silence was powerful. Satisfied that the space was ready, he called in the other dancers.

The experience was beautiful and reverent.

"*I want to dance with you,*" ushered forth out of my heart consciously unbidden.

When they finished their first dance, the head dancer announced that they were adding a dance called the Dance of Friendship.

"Dancers will come into the audience and offer a Turkey feather to some of you. If you want to dance with them, accept the Turkey feather and follow the person. If you do not want to dance, simply decline. There is no dishonor in saying no. We do not intend to embarrass anyone. If we do not ask you and you wish to dance, please come forward everyone is welcome."

The head female dancer walked directly to me and handed me her Turkey feather; I accepted it gratefully and followed her into the circle. I looked at her and asked,

"Do I get to wear one of those?" pointing to her wrists. She graciously took off a large turquoise squash blossom bracelet and gave it to me to wear. Dancing with this group felt very natural.

After the dance she did ask for the bracelet back and since then I have wanted a squash blossom bracelet of my own. With my ability to buy things wholesale, you would've thought I would have found one by now but every time I picked one up at a show and asked if it was mine, I was told '*no*'.

In Old Albuquerque, I felt drawn to the first store. I looked in the side windows and then in the front. I saw a beautiful squash blossom bracelet. My heart leapt but I feared it would be too expensive for my budget so I didn't go in. I checked out every other store and all the squash blossom bracelets were out of my budget; they started at $1000 up to $2500.

Continuing along, I was led to the local church. Inside I was guided to help a large group of souls cross over. After that was complete, I went back to the first store but instead of going in the front, I went around to the side door. I checked out different pieces in the cases and found them to be of good quality and reasonably priced, especially for being in a major tourist center. The salesclerk let me browse for a short time, then asked,

"Looking for anything specific?"

"Yes, I'm interested in a bracelet."

She went immediately to the front window and out of ten bracelets there and dozens in the store, she picked out exactly the one that lit up the first time I looked. As she brought it over to me, she said,

"This is old pawn. We have very reasonable prices on old pawn. We buy up an entire store when it's closing and we get really good deals."

She easily slipped the bracelet onto my wrist. It fit perfectly, felt good and I was reasonably certain it was not coming off.

"That doesn't usually fit without adjustment. It's surprising - it looks like it was made for you," she said. "Let me look that up and I'll tell you what the price is."

I steeled myself, expecting it to be way out of budget.

"It's one hundred fifty dollars." I removed my credit card and gave it to her before she found an extra zero.

As I walked out the front door a tall young buff bare-chested Navajo man with shining straight black hair long enough for him to sit on, was singing in his native language. He was playing a drum and bells on his ankles kept rhythm as he stepped in time to his music. I got the idea of what he was singing. He was an angry teenager singing about stupid white people who dishonor the Earth and don't understand that she is our mother.

I was drawn to him like a moth to a flame and as I listened to his entire song, we locked eyes several times. I remember feeling a bit guilty wearing the bracelet because I was not native. When he finished singing, I asked him to tell me what he was singing about to confirm what I was getting intuitively. When I asked, he gave me an odd look as if to say, '*You know what I was singing about*'. After a pause he gave a translation which confirmed my intuition. When he finished, he had his eye on my bracelet. He grabbed my arm and asked,

"Do you know why we Diné[4] (pronounced Deenay) wear turquoise?" I shook my head no.

"When we die, we Diné believe we return to the earth and we don't want to be just plain earth like this," he reached down, picked up some of the dirt and threw it down at his feet.

"We want to be turquoise. That's why turquoise is the bones of the ancestors. When you wear turquoise, you have the protection of the ancestors with you." I was feeling unworthy. He was still holding my arm and the bracelet.

"I see you are a strong woman of the earth. I was not singing to you," he said, as if he read my mind. "This bracelet is your gift and will bring you strength and protection. It is a gift of the ancestors."

He let go of my arm and I realized this was the gift the tall spirits had told me about at Mesa Verde. I said a silent prayer of gratitude and with a rush of joy energetically accepted this gift. How mysterious are the ways of spirit!

Driving back to Phoenix, I had time to think and feel again. I was firm in my stance and slightly uncomfortable realizing it now depended on what Marc's decision would be. I cried when I thought of breaking this relationship off because there was so much good. I asked for strength to hold my boundaries clearly and kindly as I drove on in silence. I had no clarity about how this would go and I tried to prepare myself for either outcome. By Phoenix I had a little internal peace about it.

---

[4] Dine is the Navajo word for Navajo. It means The People.

Chapter Thirty-Six
After Albuquerque

Marc was waiting when I returned to Phoenix.

"Let me help you with your bags. What's this?" He noticed the new bracelet.

"My gift from the tall ones."

"OK let's get you settled in and tell me all about it," he said as he carried my suitcase inside.

A beautiful bouquet of red roses was on the dining room table.

"Oh, thank you for the beautiful roses." Marc always greeted me with roses whenever I came back from a trip. I had already received more flowers from him than I received in 21 years with my ex. Marc looked for the most fragrant roses when he picked me up from the airport, knowing how much I hated the smells there. I buried my nose in the flowers as we walked through the airport.

I could feel there was a shift in his energy. I shared about the experiences of the workshop, the time shift meditation and the bracelet. I gifted him the CD purchased from the young Diné singer. It turned out to be all angry Native teenage music. You didn't have to speak the language to understand the tone.

We talked about the issues that had come up and Marc said,

"This time it is my turn to change my mind. I choose you, that is, if you will still have me."

We hugged a long time. Another relationship hurdle had been crossed. We felt closer than ever when we hugged and I felt joy, relief and gratitude. And gratitude always cycles back to create even more joy.

* * * * *

The next trip to North Carolina included working at a Body, Mind & Spirit Expo. I had a booth next to a table selling crystal bowls. Crystal bowls will bring up your issues; they entrain you to their frequency and something was coming up for me big time. It was so uncomfortable and I was trying to focus on doing readings for others.

I got someone to cover my booth and went outside out of range of the crystal bowls. Calling Marc, I asked if he was available to hold space for me. He agreed and I followed the discomfort to a lifetime in Tombstone, AZ. Marc and his brother in that lifetime, my ex this lifetime, were silver prospectors. Both were in love with me and competing for my affections. Marc managed to hit it big and jumped the claim before his brother. He also won my affections. His brother, in a jealous fit, shot at Marc and hit me in the hip, which was the area where I was feeling the most discomfort. His brother became an alcoholic and died of pneumonia alone in a cabin with little heat. I died from the wound. I felt better just knowing what this pain was about and suggested we could continue this clearing when I came back to Phoenix. I returned to the Expo and was better able to work.

When I got back to Phoenix, we went to Tombstone - and I can tell you exactly where I was shot. The pain was huge when I walked in a particular part of the town square. We sat on a bench and continued the clearing. We asked how to heal this and were guided to do a rewrite. In the rewrite Marc allowed his older brother to get the claim first. I felt the energies releasing; it felt like I was a spool of thread and someone was pulling the thread unwinding the energies from that lifetime. When the rewrite was done, neither brother had any interest in me and I felt the energy leaving.

This clearing took several days and I cried through the process, feeling that our relationship would be over after the clearing was complete. On the third day, I felt a great release and the energy between Marc and me was clearer and to my surprise, our relationship went to yet another level, a better level – a more joyful level.

Chapter Thirty-Seven
Flopped

The last house we bought to flip was a less impressive house in the North of Phoenix near where we now lived. Maria, who had financed the first two houses, asked Marc to finance this one and he did. The first day of renovations I started pulling the cigar smoke-filled carpet and didn't stop until every piece of it was at the dump. It took several full loads in the back of 'Brown Bear,' the Chevy S10 Marc had traded his beloved Subaru to get for the house flipping process. It came in handy and got great gas mileage for a truck.

It took some time to remove the popcorn ceilings, a job I recommend you get someone else to do. Much more had to be done to this house, so the reno took more time. The week before we finished, the bottom fell out of the real estate market and houses were not selling at all. The California boom was over and this house stayed on the market for months and still didn't sell. Marc had not yet found work and I was not able to support both of us and an extra mortgage.

Marc had been so busy working, traveling, flipping houses, learning to ride his long-desired motorcycle and working on our relationship that he had not spent much time on his music. He played occasionally and I especially enjoyed that. I love live music; it has a quality recorded music just can't deliver. During the lull after completing the last house, Marc was busy in his studio office for hours each day.

We had dinner together and started our Pinochle marathon. This was my family card game and we enjoyed playing double deck honeymoon Pinochle together. We were learning to communicate our feelings and developing more skills we needed to work through issues. We drew closer and closer. It was now clear we were in love and that we were headed toward a long-term relationship. We had passed many relationship hurdles including me giving up some of my favorite possessions: my down jacket, down sleeping bag and recently acquired down comforters because he was highly allergic. He called it 'the revenge of the dead geese'. His eyes would become red and he would look like he had pneumonia.

Marc kept what he was working on a secret until it was nearly a completed arrangement. Then he played this song for me:

More Than Love

The living Light that fills your face
Within this timeless, placeless place
And in your smile, a secret mirth
That builds a bridge beyond this Earth

There are no words that yet exist
To speak of how our lives have kissed
Not even Joy's resounding choir
Can fill the Grail of our desire

This is so much more
Than I had ever dreamed I could be living for
This is more than love

I want to breathe your breath within my heart
Your peace within my soul, your touch within my skin
And I believe that we shall never part
Our lives a greater Whole, the veil between so thin

Though flesh may fade in ash and dust
We rise, in pleasure's perfect Trust
Our souls' embrace, so deep and pure
Rejoined as One, as long before

Transformed by Spirit's sacred Flame
We dance where Being bears no name
Within this afterglow so sweet
Our revelation is complete

This is so much more
Than I had ever dreamed of asking Heaven for
This is more than love

I was speechless. Marc had already written me a song called *Wings* and one called *The Sound of Your Voice.* This song was on the verge of too much to take in. I was profoundly touched and wondered what I had done to deserve someone to feel so strongly about me. I was grateful but I wondered if I was worthy of so much love. Something else for me to work on. I also felt he was a step or two ahead of me as he had already often been. I was not prepared for the 'we shall never part' aspect.

"I've been thinking things over and I think I can find work in North Carolina, the job market in my field is much better there," announced Marc a few days later. "I talked with Jeff and he says I can stay with him until I find work and a house for us."

"OK, I'm open to going back," I replied, my head filling with visions of green trees and water-filled rivers. I never really felt I fit here. A system called Astrocartography looks at your astrological birth chart and superimposes it on the earth showing beneficial or challenging areas for various aspects of your life. My friend and colleague, Debra, had done mine and I was surprised at how accurate it was for things which had already happened. Phoenix was not on a line that was conducive to making money for me. The Triangle area of North Carolina was and was also good for romance and connections with others. My energy here was for spiritual development – learning more about Earth healing, deepening my meditation practices, sharpening my intuition and being able to travel to sites that needed energy work we could do together.

"Let me go first and settle in while you take care of packing up here and fixing whatever needs to be repaired before the lease is up."

"OK," I said thinking over all that would have to be done.

A day later, Marc said,

"I'm ready, I've made all the arrangements and I leave tomorrow."

"No moss grows under your feet!" I replied in surprise feeling the twinges that told me I would really miss him. I didn't expect him to depart so soon. He told me he had already applied for a few positions and wanted to be there for potential interviews. He was set. He had Brown Bear packed with the basics he would need.

A tear rolled down my cheek as I reluctantly waved goodbye in the cul-de-sac. The prospect of moving back to North Carolina brought joy. The prospect of being here alone packing did not. I tried to focus on the joy and that took work.

Chapter Thirty-Eight
Stuck in the Mud

I returned to North Carolina to see my clients and to house hunt with Marc. It was sweet to be with him and he felt so much better having found employment. We found a house that we really loved but it had gone under contract the night before. The other house we liked went into foreclosure. We were left with pretty much one house that fit our budget and needs. It was in an older community with tall trees and lovely walking paths, the first planned community for IBM people built in the 60's.

Back in Arizona, I was having a terrible time getting motivated to put things together, repair, spruce up, pack and ready for the move. It was like there was an invisible force that had created a bunch of mud and I was stuck in it knee deep. Each day was a struggle. The phone rang.

"Hello, how's it going? asked Brenda who never called me.

"To tell the truth, I'm kind of struggling here. I just don't seem to be making progress and I know I've got to get it together to move by the end of the month."

"Well, how do you feel about having some company?"

"Are you serious?" Brenda was a travelling RN and otherwise a homebody who rarely strayed more than 40 miles from her home outside Atlanta. She had probably heard from my daughter to her daughter that I was having a hard time of it or maybe that intuition of hers was working well.

"Yes, I'm serious I need a vacation. One thing I ask: can we go to the Grand Canyon?"

"I'd be happy to take you to the Grand Canyon and I would be delighted to see you and having some company for this packing would be wonderful." I was quite overwhelmed at her offer and enormously grateful. Brenda was a very practical, down to earth, let's get it done kind of person and her help would be a gift from heaven. It had also been too long since we had seen each other.

The first time I met Brenda was at a Co-op party near Philippi, West-by-God Virginia. I arrived at the party while it was in full swing and walking from my car across a field, I found a little girl in a playpen crying. No one was nearby and it looked like she had just come out of a nap. She put her arms up asking to be picked up, so I picked her up and held her close. She snuggled in like she was my own child. Pregnant at the time, my baby kicked a bit. I walked around holding this beautiful blonde-haired blue-eyed girl probably less than a year old and started talking to people in the group. This was an annual picnic and the first one I had attended.

"Who are you and do you babysit? " Was the first thing this curly brown-haired woman said to me.

"Oh, is she yours?"

"Oh yes but you're welcome to hold her if you want. She doesn't usually go to people that easily."

"She was crying in the playpen, put her arms up for me to pick her up and she just snuggled in like she knew me."

"I can see that. What is your name?"

"Lyneah."

"Oh, everybody has been telling me I need to meet you. I'm Brenda."

"Ditto, everybody has told me I need to meet you."

We chatted amiably. All the time I held Spring, the name of the young lady comfortable in my arms despite her mother's presence.

"Do you have children and I was serious about whether you babysit?"

"Only one in the oven," I rubbed my belly to accentuate my baby bump. "I'm in graduate school right now and it does not afford me much extra time especially with the amount of sleep I need now that I'm pregnant. It won't be long and I'll be interested in trading some babysitting."

Not too long after Brenda called, a friend named Pam offered to come out to help me drive back. She was interested in doing a cross country trip and also asked to see the Grand Canyon.

Seeing Brenda at Sky Harbor brought a tsunami of joy! We started packing and chatting and I got more done the first couple of days than I'd done in the two weeks prior. We waited for Pam to arrive and went to the Grand Canyon together. I was glad this would be the last time I'd have easy access to the Grand Canyon because I had been here so often, it was becoming more commonplace and the Grand Canyon should never do anything but knock your socks off.

Even though I was moving much faster with Brenda's help, Pam was impatient. The plan was Brenda would fly back a few days before I had to pack the truck. Pam and I were to share driving the truck with the car in tow. I was concerned for Goldie, my Mazda 626, because the garage that had changed out transmission fluid had not returned the plug properly and I wasn't sure if the car would make it across the country. I had only learned of this once the fluid was dangerously low and was told seals dry out rapidly in the desert. The garage that did the second repair told me to watch it closely because I might have to get a new transmission in the future. We only had two more days but Pam was antsy to get going. She insisted on taking the packed-to-the-gills Mazda and driving off by herself even after I explained my reservations.

"OK," I agreed silently asking angels to protect Pam and the car on their way. Pam left first thing early the next morning. I also prayed for radar not to catch her as she seemed in such a hurry. It turned out that she made it to her driveway in NC and the next morning the car would not move, neither forward nor backward. Goldie got her there but then the transmission gave out.

I reluctantly drove Brenda to the airport and said goodbye having enjoyed our time together. Both our daughters were young women in their 20s now and still best of friends. We had not seen each other for many years so we had much catching up to do. We hugged our goodbyes and said that we'd see each other sooner the next time. I wondered if that would happen.

"So. this relationship seems serious with Marc," Brenda observed.

"Yes, it's heading in that direction," was all I was willing to admit at this point.

When I arrived at U-Haul, they didn't have the size of truck that I had asked for. This one was several feet shorter and I was worried that everything would not fit. I had picked up some great deals at yard sales including some large pieces of furniture, so there was more going back than came out. I had a couple of friends and a strong young man from church who I hired to help with packing the truck. I started packing because I am good at that but I kept being pulled into the house with questions. The hired man was in a hurry and threw things into the truck haphazardly and I couldn't keep up. We also had Marc's recently acquired maxi scooter to get into the truck. It was by far the largest and most difficult item to pack weighing in at 500 lbs. It took three of us to walk it up the ramp. I made sure the oversized windshield was surrounded with bubble wrap and a cardboard box to protect it.

The truck ran poorly. I was beginning to think that it was on loan to U-Haul from Rent-A-Wreck. U-Haul told me that if I called around the Valley, I would not be able to find anything better and they were correct because I did make the calls. For better or worse I was stuck with this truck.

Chapter Thirty-Nine
Heading Home

With a push and a shove, we managed to get the last garden tools in and close the door. The truck was full to the max. There were things that would not fit that I gave to the people helping me. I was happy to leave Marc's microwave behind and our friend Carrie was happy to take things or find them a good home. Hugs all around. I so appreciated the people who helped. I took some of them to dinner, came home and collapsed into sleep on the floor with a sleeping bag and a pillow.

In the morning I drove out of Phoenix glad that the truck was running, all be it rough, picked up some breakfast and headed out of the Valley of the sun with Ms. Carley at my side. 87 North to Payson is a steep climb and partway up I was concerned that the truck was not going to make it. I repeatedly rocked back and forth in the driver's seat to help push it up the hill! It continued to go slower and slower. I shifted into the lowest gear and it creeped upward still losing momentum every foot of the way. Near the top I held my breath and wondered what I would do if it stopped before cresting the hill. There seemed to be something more than gravity holding me back. When I finally crested the hill, I let out a huge breath of relief. I stopped exhausted.

"Quite a beginning," I said to Ms. Carley as we walked.

We did well enough until New Mexico. I stopped in a Gallup jewelry store announcing a HUGE SALE and picked up some beautiful green Nevada turquoise pieces. One for Brenda, one for Pam and one for me. Their prices were good. I took the pieces to the checkout counter and when he told me the total price, I asked,

"Is this going to hurt you?" knowing the prices were at wholesale or below.

"We need to make rent by the 1st and we appreciate whatever sales we get," he said as he wrapped each piece and placed them in a paper bag, I carefully placed them behind the seat on Carley's side. I know I locked the truck that night but in the morning the bag of jewelry was not there. I never did find it.

It was late April and on route 40 in New Mexico I ran into every kind of weather you can imagine. We had rain, sleet, snow, ice, huge wind gusts, all rather unusual for that time of year. At one point I was on a newly paved stretch of Road in the right-hand lane with a left lane that had only been scored. The difference in pavement height was significant. Driving on the new pavement in the right lane a strong gust of wind knocked the truck over putting two wheels on the lower scored left lane and two wheels on the fresh pavement. I could feel the truck leaning and feared it would turn over on its side.

"Help!" I cried aloud to Sanat Kumara, the ancient of days, an ascended master I had been working with recently. I saw his face on the horizon. Invisible hands righted the truck. Relief and gratitude ran like rivers through me. I pulled over as soon as I could and allowed the adrenaline rush to subside before continuing.

"Hello," said Marc's voice on the other end of the telephone. "How are you coming, where are you at?"

When I told him where I was, he was concerned and mapped out how far I needed to get each day to be on schedule for getting the truck to the new house unpacked and returned within the U-Haul contract specifications.

"You have no idea how much effort it is taking me to drive this trip. I simply can't make that schedule." I cried when I told him the story of almost being knocked over on the road today and let him know that it was taking all my strength of will to drive this truck. Normally, I love driving and especially trucks but something was going on this trip that was making it difficult and exhausting.

"Well, what if I meet you somewhere along the route and help you drive?"

"That would be awesome! I would be delighted to see you and even more delighted to share this drive. It will be tight in the cab 'cause it's already pretty full and we'll have to share the passenger seat with Ms. Carley but we'll manage."

I met Marc in Little Rock, AK. His arms felt so good around me. He provided a sense of safety. He felt like a guardian. Marc suggested we call our good friend, Allysha. Together in meditation we got the idea that there were some forces that didn't want us to bring the medicine wheel across the country because it would complete a shift of a major Ley Line. We also got the idea that the cross-country lifestyle I had been living had prepared the way for this shift. The image was of an Everglades swamp boat clearing sand out of a tunnel. I carried the portal energy from the experience at Mt. Shasta and by simply going back and forth it had cleared. We asked for help and protection from Angels and spirit guides and the rest of the trip went easier. I felt the power of two multiplied our strength.

Marc and I conversed easily glad to be doing so without the aid of a cell phone. We caught up on general things like his new job at UNC and the time with Brenda and Pam. I told him we would have to tow Goldie and have her transmission replaced. Being his considerate self, he offered to have me drive him to work so I could use Brown Bear while Goldie was in the shop. We had placed the flipper house in the hands of a realtor as it had not yet sold. We talked about creating a treatment room in the Durham house and the possibilities for other work for me. We were now homeowners together, a major step in our relationship.

"Would you marry me?" asked Marc.

"I'm allergic to marriage. I will stay with you and love you but the institution of marriage is not one I am interested in." Two ugly divorces in my past I was not interested in getting into another marriage. I watched Marc negotiate his divorce with admiration and wished mine had been as civilized. He and his ex still talked with respect and were able to be friends, which I found foreign but applauded. I simply wasn't ready for marriage nor did I think I would ever be.

"This is not personal." I tried comforting him. But he still looked rejected.

Chapter Forty
Hugged by a House?

It was a relief to be back in familiar territory. The truck made it up the steep driveway taking a chunk of pavement with it as it went. We hired someone to help us move in. Ms. Carley was happy to have a path to walk in the mornings. We thought the bamboo forest in the back of our property was cool but this very invasive species turned out to be a problem. The neighbors were big Duke supporters. They had moved into their house in the late 60's with a red Corvette and I always imagined him in a letterman sweater and her in a cheerleader outfit despite their ages.

When things quieted down, I sat in the meditation chair in our new living room. This room was big enough to hold classes and gatherings, one of the reasons for choosing this house, or maybe it chose us. All the other houses that interested us were not available at the time we had to buy. The cute house with the sky lights came back on the market too late for us to back out of this one. I had to believe Spirit had reasons why this house and not the other.

We did a clearing. The house had been owned by one family since it was built. The man, who planted the two stalks of bamboo despite the objections of the neighbors, had passed. His widow had been moved to a nursing home and the house had been rented out to a family that abused it. We completed clearing the negative energy left behind and elevating the energies to ones that would support us and our work. Marc and I worked side by side in this process and it felt so right.

Later, something in the middle of the house made me feel we had made a mistake. Marc was at work, so I called Maria for help. Together we identified a vortex of energy that needed to be cleared and shifted. Upon completion the house felt safe and comfortable.

I went to the meditation chair in need of some quiet time. I did my opening and just sat in stillness grateful to be here. I felt a sweet energy different from anything I had felt before. It came around me like a sweet hug. It was a wonderful energy to enjoy. I was curious.

"Who is this?" I asked.

"I'm your house," came the response. *"I'm so glad you are here. The last people did not appreciate me and you are different."*

I felt we would be happy together and I wondered what adventures being here would bring. In meditation I asked and saw a tableau of images. Students learning earth healing here and trips Marc and I would take. Trips I would take alone. Two weddings and one included me in a wedding dress! I was no longer the same person who left. I had learned so much and grown in so many ways in the desert. I hoped that the growth would continue.

"We'll see," I thought and went back to enjoying the connection with our new house for a few more minutes before returning to the unpacking process. The connection with the house was one of pure joy.

Thirsting for more joy in my life I had learned that joy was not just something that spontaneously happens, it is something we create for ourselves. Make more joy for others and you will experience more joy yourself. Gratitude is also a guaranteed method of having more joy. The more truly heartfelt gratitude I created by reviewing the amazing things that happened, the more joy I experienced. I had to let my heart soar. I reflected on how far my life had come from the anger filled last days of my previous marriage.

It had been two years and six months since my first visit to Phoenix! So much had happened! I asked Spirit,

"Why did I have to take all my furniture across the country when I would only be there less than three years?"

"We didn't expect you to do it all in this short a time."

"When you give me an assignment in the desert, I'm going to jump on it and get it done as fast as possible. I am grateful for the experiences and the learning and joyously grateful to be back where there trees are green and go colorful in the fall and rivers that have water year-round."

170

Ms. Carley put her head in my lap and I pet her glad for her company.

"Well Ms. Carley, I wonder what our next adventures will be?" Her wagging tail told me she was also happy to be here and she was always ready for adventure. Marc seemed to be ready for an adventure all the time. I was learning to embrace this attitude toward life and he seemed to be a great partner for this. The most important thing I learned was to listen to Spirit with discernment and trust. Trust that we would be guided to do our work in the world.

I fell into a deep receptive meditation and saw visions. Many flashed by so fast I didn't catch them and others were brief impressions: a wedding and I was wearing black, another wedding where I was wearing a platinum color, a walk on a beautiful tropical beach, several other walks on beaches, a huge snow-covered mountain, a beautiful blue sea, a castle.

"*What does this mean*?" I asked Spirit.

"*You'll see.*"

Chapter Forty-One
Interview

The following is the beginning of an interview that was done after the pre-release of this book.

"I'm so glad you agreed to do this interview. I find your book fascinating but I have so many questions," Marion began the interview.

"I'm happy to be here and interested in knowing what you want to know?" I replied.

"Let's get right to it then, I think my first question is why did you write this book?"

"Ah, good question. I wrote this book because I was guided to and because I was told in meditations that it could inspire others. I want people to see that an ordinary life can become extraordinary when you turn it over to Spirit, your Higher Self, God, Divine Source, Great Spirit -- whatever you want to call that higher power -- and follow your intuition. I did that after my near-death experience way back in 1975. I was 25 years old then and the experience so dramatically changed the trajectory of my life. I've been tempted on occasion to rescind that permission but I have not. Willingness is a big key to living this kind of life. Willingness when it makes no logical sense. Willingness when your family looks at you askance. Willingness when you don't really want to, like me and the desert. "

"Yes, your willingness is impressive. I believe it has inspired many, I know it inspired me. When I read it, I believe this is what Jean Houston calls the heroine's journey."

"Yes, that was in one of the jacket quotes on the first book. Jean's former assistant, Fonda Joyce called it that in her book review.

During my near-death experience (NDE), my grandfather indicated it was important that I get back here and live my life. He indicated strongly there were things I needed to do and I was determined to find out what they were and, to the best of my ability, do them."

"How long did it take you to write?"

"I started the first book, *Thirsting for A Raindrop*, a number of years ago and it took me about two years. I had a great deal of resistance to telling the metaphysical stories and was reluctant to tell the story of my divorce. My resistance has reduced greatly over the years. *Thirsting for Joy* happened several years later but took much less time; the first 23 chapters were drafted, edited and formatted within two weeks! The energy of Mt. Shasta helped. It was also a case of the stars aligning and the time being right. It was winter, so hibernation felt like a good thing to do. Also, it was during the pandemic which gave most of us more at home time."

"That's amazing. Did you do anything else during that time?"

"Yes, I had a few client consults and snow to shovel and I could not sit all the time writing. I have a regular phone work out appointment three mornings a week with my niece who is also a great listener. She was the first-read person and helped me smooth out the edges . My husband, Marc, was the first editor and I am so grateful for his help. Fonda listened to the edited version. I think you could say writing the two books was the difference between paddling upstream and flowing downstream."

"I'd say you struck while the iron was hot."

"Indeed."

"Are all these stories true?"

"Yes, they are - and there are more I haven't told yet. I've changed some names or details to protect people but the stories are true. A few words have been created to make a point where the actual words were not in my memory but I remembered the gist of the conversation. I understand your question. Sometimes when I read it, I wonder if I lived it. I thought about publishing it as sci-fi but that was not my guidance. It would have been much easier to hide behind the veil of science-fiction. Yet life is supposed to be amazing for anyone who choses this type of path. Everyone's details will differ of course, as we all have different gifts and talents."

"How did you learn to listen to your intuition so clearly?"

"That was actually quite a long process involving dedication and work. I was born with what Rudolph Steiner calls atavistic intuition, one that is automatic -- possibly earned in past lives. I started consciously asking for help to learn how to meditate when I first lived in West Virginia shortly after the near-death experience. There was no one teaching meditation there at that time, so I read some books, sat under a particular dogwood tree overlooking the Laurel Mountains five miles away and started applying what I had read. It was a peaceful beautiful spot and I just sat. I did some breathing exercises, connected with the earth, worked at quieting my mind - what they call the monkey mind, the one that's chattering all the time if you don't train it to be still.

I was living a simple, back-to-earth life at that time, living in a tent way back in the woods. My neighbors were cows, deer, a beautiful red fox and a grandaddy gopher. I had an outdoor kitchen and loved my lifestyle. I did that for eight months. My work was digging and building a stone foundation for a stack log home. The plan was to make it solar tempered and partially dug in. I read Paramahansa Yogananda's *Autobiography of a Yogi*. I did something called a word fast, not speaking for several weeks, using an erase board when I had to communicate. That was a powerful discipline and meditation. I also read Baba Ram Dass' *Be Here Now*, which I found inspiring. Later he came to Morgantown and I got to meet him and listen to him in person.

Every morning started with meditation, which was more of a non-doing than a doing. Yearning in my heart for a teacher to help me, one day I felt a spirit next to me. I asked discernment and he remained, so I knew he was there for my highest good and was the answer to my request. He was an older Indian gentleman with white hair, who suggested ways that I could start meditating more deeply. I followed his instructions daily. One day he told me that I was ready to learn walking meditation, gave me instructions that after I reached a deep state of meditation, I would stand up and start

177

consciously walking, placing toe – middle foot - heel and then lifting the other foot in a threefold way, continuing to walk consciously while in a state of meditation."

"Do you know who this man was?"

"It's funny, I never asked his name at the time. I had used my method of discernment and I knew that he was beneficial; that was enough for me. If someone wants to go along this path, all you do is ask for the person who is right for you and s/he will either show up in the physical or in the spiritual - just use your form of discernment to make sure that the person is there for your highest good and for the highest good of all. When you are ready the teacher comes."

"Well, I think that's good advice no matter what you're doing, isn't it?"

"It is one of the first things I teach in my classes: center and align with Divine Source, then ask what right action is. And when I've used this method, it has kept me out of trouble. When I haven't is when I've had problems like the story about the kidney stone or any number of the stories in the thread in the next book called 'Be careful what you ask for."

"So, using discernment keeps you out of trouble."

"Not always, it sometimes takes me into interesting circumstances but when I continue to ask, I get guidance and the help I need to complete the task. Like the earthquake time you read about in this book."

"Earthquake. Yes, that was an intense moment. So, there's a third book in the making?

"Yes, I have started the third book."

"Last time we talked, you were saying your stories are intended to inspire," Marian began.

"Yes, today I was participating in a Stargate Meditation with Prageet and Julianne. Prageet channels Alcazar, a representative of a group of beings helping the Earth ascend. You can find out more about them at www.stargateexperienceacademy.com. Today he was encouraging participants to share their stories because *'...the more we share the magic, the more we can allow the magic to happen for us. Hearing other people's magic can touch our inner knowing, part of ourselves that we have forgotten about. Our connectedness to Spirit in a way we are not using, not manifesting to the depth and the height that we could...'* I hope the stories I share in my books will do just that, stimulate your inner knowing and awaken the connection to Spirit that you know inside is there for you. I have become a Certified Stargate Facilitator and do regular meditations online. Anyone interested can apply to join through email, Lyneahmarks@bodysoulandangels.com.

"That's really interesting. I think that works if the person reading is intending that to happen."

"Exactly. There are spiritual downloads available in these books and if you intend to receive them you will. You will receive the ones that are perfect for you at this time. Many people like to read one chapter before bed and allow the downloads to happen in sleep."

"That's efficient. On another subject, let me see if I have the right sequence of you and Marc meeting. You met at a Jean Houston Mystery School in upstate New York; he was in Boston and you in Durham, North Carolina."

"That's right."

"He moved to Arizona and you were invited by a friend he didn't even know to come to Arizona."

"Yes, that's correct."

"You received direction to move to Arizona even though you were almost phobic about deserts."

"I wouldn't say almost."

"Yet you moved."

"Sure, why not? My daughter had moved to Atlanta, I had no relatives in the Durham area except my older brother, who was happily married and had his own life. I did have many friends, colleagues and clients but I knew that my support had moved and I had to follow. Don't get me wrong, I had free choice. I could have stayed but my life would not have been nearly as interesting. Probably my practice would have dwindled and I would not have had the magic in my life to which I was growing accustomed. My guidance would have been slowed if not stopped."

"It seems a very brave thing to do, getting up and moving across the country."

+ "It was just part of how I chose to live my life by following my internal guidance. It seems to me it would have taken a lot more strength to have resisted the guidance and in the past when I resisted my guidance major things have happened. My NDE was a one. The burning of our instrument building shop for another."

"Isn't that outside free will then?"

"Absolutely not! I had given Spirit permission to guide me, so that was my free will and if I had contracts that were made before I came into this life, they were also made out of free will. I came here for a purpose or a series of purposes I guess."

"Isn't there someone else who can fulfill that purpose?" Marian asked.

"Sometimes there is and sometimes there isn't. Rudolph Steiner said he came to spiritualize science but the person who had come to spiritualize education shirked his contract and Steiner had to shift into that role. Some say he is back now to spiritualize science.

"At one point, after we finished a dramatic healing for a friend, I asked what would have happened had I not answered Spirit's call that day and the answer was,

'There was no one else available in that time or place.'

I find it scary when I realize my willingness to do something can so strongly affect the course of someone else's life but it is also a strong motivator to listen and follow. What I find is that if something is important, I get very strongly pushed to do it - sometimes actually physically. This past year, I was participating in online Stargate meditations and enjoying them quite a bit; toward the end of one series Prageet announced spaces had opened in the upcoming Stargate Facilitator's training. *"That's nice,"* I thought. A firm hand at my back pushed me forward and I heard the emphatic word, *"Apply!!!"*

I went to the computer, applied and a few weeks later I had become a Certified Stargate Facilitator."

"Is that story in one of your books?"

"Not yet, possibly in the next one."

"Do you think everyone has such contracts?"

"Probably not everyone. There are those who have come to help at this time in history and have such contracts. But I could not speak for everyone."

"Is it always dramatic fulfilling your destiny?"

"No, often it's simple and sometimes boring. I've been told to go places and just sit for hours because my energy was needed there. Or we are told to drive and drive and drive in the space of a few days and I can feel energy running through me but those situations don't generally make good stories."

"I can see that. If we feel we have such contracts and have not started working on them, where can we start?"

"Set your intention to learn what you need to. Set your heart to a path of service, whether that's your main job or a sideline. If you want to develop your intuition, Rudolph Steiner's Five Basic Exercises, which you can download off my website free:

www.bodysoulandangels.com/meditation

They are an excellent place to begin. These exercises are designed to be safe for everyone if you do not do them for selfish reasons and if you are patient with yourself. The kind of patience is the kind that knows our efforts can span several lifetimes meaning you might not see the results until the next lifetime but you have to continue to practice the exercises knowing you will see results and generally, they manifest quickly."

"If you want to study with me, contact me."

"I just want to say a huge thank you to my husband who edited and re-edited. Thank you for putting up with me my love. Also, my niece who listened carefully twice through and provided great questions, comments and suggestions. She has a great ear. Also, great gratitude to all my clients and friends who have encouraged me to write. Thank you for your patience those of you who have been waiting for the second book. I hope you enjoy it. I also offer gratitude to my Mother who raised me the best way she knew how, didn't always understand me but always loved me. Love you and miss you in the physical Mom."

Every moment that we spend in higher consciousness helps uplift the consciousness of the whole world.

I would happily offer credit to whoever put this beautiful piece together but I don't know who to credit. Thank you for providing inspiration.

About the Author

Lyneah Marks currently lives in Mt. Shasta, CA where she is working on the sequel to this book entitled, *Thirsting for More*. Lyneah works as a healer doing personal Soul Integration Sessions on phone and Zoom, facilitates individual and group Stargate Meditations, and teaches classes. Her website, www.Bodysoulandangels.com, contains information on her various services and events. She also hosts and facilitates Stargate Meditations on Zoom. She has expanded her earth healing work and many of these stories will appear in *Thirsting for More*.

Hi, Lyneah here. If you enjoyed this book, I'd greatly appreciate your positive review on Amazon or other sites and I would love to hear from you: Lyneahmarks@bodysoulandangels.com.

To learn about events, classes, meditations and healing sessions,
contact Lyneah.

FOR YOUR SPECIAL GIFT KEEP GOING

183

Keep going…

A SPECIAL BONUS GIFT FROM LYNEAH

Do you feel inspired by these stories? Do you want more magic and miracles in your life? Would you like to clear blocks that have been stopping you from doing what your heart desires? Are you ready to follow Spirit's call in new and bigger ways?

Would you like to feel more in control of your life? MY GIFT to you, as a reader of this book and as a first-time client, is a special introductory Soul Integration session for **HALF OFF!** This session can be done via phone or zoom.

Just email me at **LyneahGift@gmail.com** and I'll send the details. Include **JOY 50% OFF** in the subject line. Use discernment -- ask your guidance if this is for you. Will it serve your highest good?

What are people saying about Soul Integration Healing Sessions? See the next page.

I look forward to working with you.

May you find greater and greater joy!

TESTIMONIALS

"I have worked with many healers, yet Lyneah Marks exceeds just about all of them with her gifts. In one session we cleared so much past life trauma that had been lodged in my energy body and blocking me from completely healing from some serious illness. Since that session, my mood and my energy has lifted incredibly and my body is making huge strides towards full health. I absolutely love Lyneah's incredible work and know that anyone can benefit from one session or more with her. Thank you, Lyneah!"   Mare Cromwell, author of The Great Mother Bible

"One session with you changed my life profoundly for the better!"
Durham, NC

"One of the most profound changes for me resulting from the Soul Integration work is a greater body awareness and the connections between discomfort in my physical body and emotional states which need to be healed. I had a chronic shoulder injury two years before working with Lyneah and she has gotten it mostly clear. When it causes me pain now, I know I have another level of emotional healing to do and I call Lyneah. The physical healing is minor compared to the soul-spiritual healing which has been deep and profound."   Mary Baird, Personal trainer, Durham, NC

"Lyneah is a healer's healer."   Mt. Shasta, CA

"Thank you Lyneah, I would not have made it through this chaos (complex and nasty divorce) to the other side without your love, support and guidance. I have a new life — new adventure in front

of me and I am so much happier! I can't wait to see you next time."
A long-term client

"I have 'experienced' Lyneah's healing work over the course of several years. The depth and breadth of her vocational training, innate wisdom, and genuine compassion melded with her guru instinct have helped me 'to help myself' on all levels. Lyneah, with her heightened guidance and the practical techniques she imparts, is my favorite healing facilitator. We have cleared roadblocks along my path to love and oneness, traveling together. She is truly enlightened and a universal blessing!"
Corey DeAhna CloverFox

"Lyneah is a gifted healer with the ability to help people perceive the ways in which their spiritual growth has been hindered and to guide souls to feel again the real presence of God's love that is their ultimate healer. I have greatly benefited from her services and highly recommend her to those who wish to similarly benefit."
Glen Cotton

"Each session was a great teaching session for me as a healer. Lyneah lifts me to a higher dimension. I am seeing visions more clearly. Lyneah opened the Akashic records for me and now I can see them on my own. I have learned techniques which profoundly change the energy of my past lives. Each session I have opened up to more clarity, more empowerment, and a deeper spiritual awareness. You have brought out in me the potentials that are really there -- ones that I didn't even know about. I never knew you could go this far with the work. I am at a higher level. Lyneah is an awesome healer and a great teacher. Fully open to the possibilities of me being my best and all that is for the highest good."
Gisela Arenas, Quantum Angel Healing Practitioner,   Tempe, AZ

See what Soul Integration can do for you. Just email me at LyneahGift@gmail.com and I'll send the details. Include 50% OFF OFFER in the subject line. New Clients Only

For more testimonials see www.bodysoulandangels.com/testimonials

Body Soul & Angels Publishing

Made in the USA
Middletown, DE
24 July 2021